Broken Whole

HEALING A SHATTERED HEART
THROUGH DIVINE LOVE
AND UNBREAKABLE FAITH

Christy Droog

Broken Whole

Healing a Shattered Heart Through Divine Love and Unbreakable Faith

© 2023, Christy Droog.

Print ISBN: 979-8-35092-539-5

eBook ISBN: 979-8-35092-540-1

Dedication

I lovingly dedicate this book to my son, Gabriel and my mom, Emmy.

I love you both to Infinity and beyond!

Contents

Foreword

by Deborah King

In *Broken Whole*, memoirist Christy Droog movingly excavates and unravels her shocking personal history—abandoned at birth, a sexual abuse victim at age 5, an unwed mother at 19, by age 22 she was scarred by a failed marriage and the tragic drowning of her infant son. Soon after, divorced and facing the loss of her mother to cancer, Christy finds herself in a full-blown spiritual crisis, grasping at the eternal questions we all ask: *What is my purpose? Why is God not listening to my pleas, my prayers? Does God even love me?*

In these pages, documenting her near-nervous breakdown and multiple life-threatening surgeries, Christy bravely chronicles her harrowing quest to resolve this spiritual unease, to dredge through the past and to find the answers. Will her courageous attempts to build a positive path, to strive for a better future, and to satisfy her questions about womanhood, motherhood and faith lead her to freedom, to a reawakening, to release?

A rare and unflinching look at the power of love to overcome and transcend loss, *Broken Whole* takes readers on a spiritual voyage of personal transformation. Intensely personal, and universally human, it is the story of one woman's journey into her own life, and a meditation on the questions that challenge us all.

SCARS

*Out of suffering have emerged the strongest souls; the
most massive characters are seared with scars.*

~ Khalil Gibran

Broken Whole was born from my personal journey of transforming my physical, emotional, mental, and spiritual suffering into a Wholeness I never dreamed was possible and sharing that Wholeness with others. From the broken and shattered parts of my life, I fashioned Wholeness by mixing them with a type of gold that drew all these pieces back together into a more beautiful and complex system. This gold was comprised of my scars combined with unconditional love.

My life story is etched onto my scars, both visible and hidden. They bear witness to the challenges I have encountered, the losses I have suffered, the traumas I have endured, and every victory only a Higher Power could have orchestrated. I may have been battered and bruised by the rocky road I walked to find the light within, but I am not broken. And I am not alone.

Neither are you.

Ultimately, scars become wisdom.

They teach us forgiveness.

They teach us compassion.

They teach us love.

And *Love*; love is the way back to wholeness.

As a young child, as early as five years old, I felt drawn to the idea of healing and helping others. It was as if something deep within me knew that this was my path. I practiced my "nursing skills" on anyone who would let me, and I felt a sense of purpose and fulfillment in caring for others. As I grew older, my desire to become a nurse only intensified. I wanted to be part of the healing process, to make a difference in people's lives.

And so, I pursued my dream, working hard to graduate from nursing school and become a Registered Nurse. For over 20 years, I have dedicated myself to helping others as a Home Care Case Manager. But my journey didn't end there. In recent years, I discovered a passion for end-of-life care and began exploring holistic approaches to healing.

In July of 2012, my journey took a transformative turn as I delved into the realm of energy healing, bridging the gap between traditional nursing and a more holistic approach to care. This experience brought to light the critical importance of viewing individuals as a complete entity, rather than just a set of symptoms or ailments.

Of course, at age 5, I had no idea the challenges I would need to over-come along my jagged path to becoming a nurse and a healer. These events would shape me to become the best version of myself.

Encountering difficulty in life is inevitable, and I've yet to meet anyone who hasn't experienced some type of adversity. Trauma—whether physical, emotional, mental, or spiritual—becomes an open wound. Those wounds bleed. But eventually, wounds heal, forming scars. Scars prove we have suf-fered an injury and overcome the pain and trauma of the original soul-pierc-ing wound. Though it might seem ugly or painful; eventually, a beautiful masterpiece is revealed. Scars help us relate to and connect with others in ways we never thought possible. Ultimately, we learn to live from the scar instead of the broken pieces.

A warrior doesn't hide her scars. Her scars are symbols of courage, shouts of victory. They symbolize the battlegrounds she has walked, the battles she has faced, the wars she has survived and won, and the triumph from the gift of Divine healing.

Though it hasn't always been the case in my journey, I feel at peace with my scars today. In the past, every new scar wounded a piece of my heart, and now I embrace them—even love them. Each scar offers me a glimmer of recovery; some remind me that I have survived the un-survivable. Only now do I see every broken piece of my bruised and broken heart as part of a much larger picture. Embracing the fractured elements of my life, lovingly gluing them back together, creating an even more robust, more beautiful version of myself. The one I use today to help others do the same.

I am grateful that the whole picture was not revealed to me all at once; that was Divine planning. Had I known what I was about to endure, I wouldn't have had the courage to face it, walk it, and live through it.

My healing and spiritual journey merged those shattered pieces and my beauty marks. I see my scars in a new light, restored with purpose.

Prologue

THE SPARK OF LIGHT

The tiny Spark of Light,
filled with excitement and wonder,
whispered in the ear of the Divine Mother,
"I'm ready!"

Concealing her tears, The Divine Mother responded.
"Little Spark, the Path will be hard.
You will know sorrow and loss, abandonment and betrayal."

The Spark replied,
"I know, but I will also experience beauty, awe, joy, and love!
I will bring with me Heaven on earth!"

The Divine Mother smiled and said,
"My dear child,
Go on your way...
Soon you will find yourself in the comfort of your mother's womb.
I've chosen one who will heed the call for selfless giving and surrender.
Remember, no matter what, to look deep into your heart.
When life becomes difficult as often it does,
Always remember the Spark of Light that you are,
Everything you'll ever need to know already exists within you.

Many will cross your path needing the touch of your gentle heart.
Be not hardened by your experiences,
Instead, grow in Wisdom, Compassion and Love.
Remember to shine your bright Light even on the darkest of nights.
Illuminate their hearts with your Inner Light,
sparking their own Remembrance.
The Journey ahead may seem lonely at times,
But always remember you are never Alone.
Do not look outside for what you seek most
I have placed a secret jewel sealed inside your heart.
Your destiny is to remember.
Seek, and you shall discover your treasure."

The tiny Spark beamed at the Divine Mother.
Putting a hand to her heart, she reassured,
"Yes, Mama, I will remember...."

Prelude

SHATTERED

With tears streaming down her cheeks, the nurse gently placed my lifeless son in my arms.

This moment would forever be etched into my soul as a painful wound that I wasn't sure could ever heal. Gabriel was a part of me, and I had carried him in my womb. I witnessed this incredible extension of myself grow and flourish for two and a half years. And now, that part of me was dead.

My heart lay shattered into a million pieces on the cold hospital floor. This was the moment that changed the entire trajectory of my life. I had known grief before, but this event is the one that shook me to the core of my whole being. The death of my child took me to the deepest and darkest part of my soul, leaving me unsure if I could ever return.

Nothing could have prepared me for this unbearable pain.

Chapter One

CAGED

I was 19.

Shame tied my stomach into knots as I watched the timer count down to zero. Desperately I stared at the clock, hoping for a miracle. *How could this be happening?*

As the timer buzzed, my heart stopped. I plucked up the plastic stick with a deep hopeful breath, praying I would see a negative result. Suddenly my stomach clutched, and I sobbed as I caught a glimpse of the pregnancy test result.

Positive. I'm pregnant!? I stared in shock. *Now what?* Instantly, my mind replayed every action that led to this moment.

I was raised better than this; I scolded myself. *I knew better!* I had gone against every one of my instincts and faith out of fear of being alone and abandoned again.

And by going against my faith and myself, it felt like the positive pregnancy test was well-deserved punishment for my careless actions.

Throughout my life, faith has played an essential role in shaping who I am and what I believe. Growing up attending St. Michael's Catholic Church and School allowed me to develop a deep connection to my faith and a belief in the power of angels. The experience of singing in the choir and participating in worship music provided me with a sense of community that was irreplaceable.

One of the fundamental teachings of my faith was to wait until marriage before being intimate with someone. I always believed in this teaching and felt confident that it was the right path for me. However, as I entered University, I found myself faced with a new set of challenges and temptations that made it much more difficult to stick to this belief. The temptation to give in to my desires became increasingly strong, and I found myself struggling to reconcile my faith with my desires.

Living away from my parents for the first time, I embraced the excitement of city life but missed the familiarity of my rural hometown and family farm. My boyfriend provided me with a sense of belonging and security that I yearned for, but my internal conflict between my desires and beliefs left my heart in turmoil. The thought of intimacy secretly enticed me, and the affection from my boyfriend felt gratifying. I struggled between upholding my values or pursuing the relationship further.

Ultimately, my fear of losing him was more significant than my fear of being judged, and I ended up betraying my beliefs.

I hoped to keep it a secret, but the reality hit home as I looked at the positive pregnancy test, and soon, there would be no more hiding.

Upon discovering my pregnancy, I was overwhelmed with fear and uncertainty. I knew my parents had to be told in person, and the thought filled me with dread. How could I break this news without causing them shame and disappointment?

As my boyfriend and I drove to my parent's farm to break the news, my anxiety consumed me. The pit in my stomach grew, and I felt like a complete failure. *How could I have let this happen? How could I have betrayed the values that had been instilled in me since childhood?*

As we pulled up to the farm, I could feel my parents' eyes on us, and I knew they could sense that something was wrong. The walk from the car to the front door felt like an eternity, and I wanted to turn back, run away, and disappear into thin air.

The conversation with my parents was difficult. They were disappointed and hurt, and I felt every bit of their emotions. I could see the blame in their eyes, and it only made me feel worse. I felt like I had let them down and that I had somehow tarnished their reputation in our small town.

My mother couldn't help but take some of the blame. She recounted how she had thrown out my birth control pills months earlier out of frustration with my mood swings and symptoms. She felt that her actions, combined with her absence during a vacation, had contributed to my decision to have sex.

My father, though disappointed, was immediately focused on finding a solution. He began asking us what our plans were moving forward and what we could do to prepare for the arrival of our child. Even in the midst of disappointment and hurt, he was determined to support us.

It was a difficult day, but their love and support helped me begin to find a way forward.

We knew that we had three options to consider: abortion, adoption, or keeping the baby. The choice ahead of us was difficult, and we had to weigh the pros and cons of each option carefully.

Initially, my first thought was to have an abortion. It seemed like the most convenient way to eliminate the problem and avoid shame or embarrassment from facing my community. It would allow me to continue my college education without any interruption from pregnancy or having to care for a child.

Adoption was off the table—much to my parents' bewilderment. I couldn't bear the thought of giving up my child to someone else. The wound of abandonment I had suffered since my own birth prevented me from being willing to offer my child the same fate. Despite the gratitude I felt for my chance at life, I wasn't willing to put my child in the same position I had been in. Placing the child for adoption immediately after birth was the option both my boyfriend and I were against.

The thought of keeping the baby and raising it terrified me. The responsibility I would have to take on was more than I could bear. I didn't have a clue how to be a mother! Wrestling with the problems of being a teenage girl was hard enough. I was in a true crisis; it would lead to feeling pressured into marriage to right my wrongdoing. Another thought I had not entertained was becoming a mother—and possibly a wife—while finishing University. Changing diapers while studying had never been part of my plan. Considering this now overwhelmed me.

This made the choice easy. Abortion would be my path.

Devastated at the possibility of an abortion, my Dad set up an appointment with our local Birthright to discuss other options. Choosing abortion from my parent's perspective was a punch in the gut of epic proportions. Unable to conceive their own biological children, they could not understand how I could entertain the notion of not bringing the baby growing in my belly to life. Being adoptive parents was one of their greatest gifts; they remained hopeful I would make the same decision if I felt I couldn't keep the baby myself. I wasn't persuaded to reconsider my options and decided to follow through with setting plans for the abortion in place.

A week later, waiting impatiently in the sitting area for my appointment time at the sexual health center, anticipating the end date for this nightmare, I felt a knot tighten in my stomach. *Just a little while longer, and then you are free,* I thought to myself. I could almost taste the relief of knowing this pregnancy chapter was about to be closed. *And no one will ever know.*

Suddenly I felt sick to my stomach. My heart started pounding; it felt like an elephant was sitting on my chest. It was hard to breathe. Sweat dripped from my shaky hands. The room I was sitting in became dead silent. *What am I doing here? This doesn't feel right.* What had felt like the sure decision was now uncertain. Despite my desire to hide my shame, I knew in my heart of hearts I couldn't go through with it.

As I walked out of the building, filled with trepidation, I knew my path was leading me in another direction.

By process of elimination, that left only one option: Keep the baby. I felt defeated; a sense of doom flooded my being. Desperately, for weeks, I wished away the pregnancy. I prayed for a miscarriage. I'd sit, my heart quivering with grief, wanting to punch my stomach but unable to bring myself—or the baby—that kind of pain.

For reasons only God knows, getting a free pass was not in the cards. I carried my baby to term. As the pregnancy progressed, I adjusted to the idea once I firmly decided to keep the baby and realized the pregnancy would remain viable. I was still scared, but somehow I knew I had everything I needed inside myself and would be able to handle it all.

For me, pregnancy was a time of complete agony rather than delight, as it is for many women. I didn't have the cute, round belly and blushing glow others seemed to have. Instead, I gained 60 pounds due to severe water retention and developed high blood pressure. I needed eight weeks of bed rest before giving birth and suffered from daily vomiting and exhaustion throughout the pregnancy. I felt miserable and loathed my appearance. Looking in the mirror, I saw a grotesque, swollen woman that made me question how anyone could love me. Somehow, my boyfriend still did; this gave me a glimmer of hope. But loving myself was impossible.

A shocking scene unfolded before me one evening at a local restaurant with my father and boyfriend. Their quiet conversation erupted into tense words, then into a furious and bitter argument over whether my boyfriend dared to do the right thing and marry me. A pit formed in my stomach, and the room became blurred. No one had asked *me* if I wanted to get married!

The romantic dream of a marriage proposal at the Eiffel Tower that I had envisioned since childhood instantly evaporated, leaving me feeling like an item at an auction, sold to the highest bidder.

I sat there silently, listening to their angry words reverberating in my head, unable and unwilling to stand up for myself. I had long ago lost my voice and surrendered to the dominance of the strong male presences in my life. Whenever conflict arose, I would shrink myself to avoid being seen and allow others to make decisions for me.

Weeks later, as I lay on the couch, exhausted from pregnancy, my boyfriend pulled out a catalogue. He pointed out a picture of an engagement ring and asked, "Do you like it?" I shrugged. Half joking, half serious, I answered, "I would want a bigger diamond."

Quickly he disappeared downstairs and returned with a box, clumsily setting it in front of me. Shocked, I opened the box to see the same diamond engagement ring I had just dismissed. I didn't know what to say. I felt tricked. I felt guilty that speaking my truth had ruined my own engagement and made him feel inadequate all at the same time. Out of guilt, I insisted we keep the ring—but it wasn't what I truly wanted. Why would I speak my truth if it only hurt me even more?

And so, the plans for our wedding began. I took on the role of a silent observer. Inside, I wanted to scream. I loved him, but I wasn't ready to marry! *I am only 19!* I kept reminding myself. An unspoken understanding hung in the air—I was pregnant, and now I had to pay the price. My voice, already weak, already timid, became nonexistent. Stewing with resignation, I allowed my Mom to choose my wedding dress.

It all felt so wrong. The ring and the dress. The wedding. My whole life.

This was not how I had envisioned what was supposed to be one of the happiest occasions of my life.

I'd always dreamed of a June wedding. However, I was due to deliver the baby in July. When I voiced this, my Mom placed her hands around her pretend-pregnant belly mockingly and snickered, "Here comes the bride!" This stung me to my core. Unwilling to wait until the following spring, my boyfriend insisted we marry no later than the end of November, four months after the arrival of our precious little one. *That's fine,* I sighed, surrendering. Arguing was pointless. Consequently, I chose the last possible date in November and gave up my dream of a springtime wedding.

Complicating the choice of a wedding date was our local church priest—he was unwilling to baptize our baby until we were married. Irate, I barely contained my fury. *Why would the church punish my child, and deny my genuine desire to have our child baptized, because of my "sin"?*

My faith had always been a guiding force in my life, giving me strength and solace during difficult times. But now, as I faced the reality of my situation, I couldn't help but question the teachings I had been raised with. Was the Church really the embodiment of faith, or was it false too?

As I struggled to come to terms with these conflicting beliefs, I couldn't help but feel a sense of separation from religion. It was as if I had been cut adrift, no longer anchored by the comforting embrace of my faith. And yet, even in this moment of doubt and uncertainty, I couldn't shake the belief in a forgiving God.

It seemed unjust and cruel to punish my child for my own mistakes. *Would a loving God condone such a thing?* As these thoughts swirled in my head, I realized that my belief in a compassionate and merciful deity was at odds with the teachings of the Church.

Despite this realization, I held on to the hope that there was more to faith than what I had been taught. Perhaps, somewhere out there, there was a place where forgiveness and compassion were the guiding principles.

While I struggled with my internal dilemma, my unborn baby was thriving and getting closer to entering the world. As the due date approached, my emotions became more complex. When I was alone, I would catch a glimpse of my growing belly, and for brief moments, my feelings of guilt would dissipate. In those instances, I would smile faintly, marvelling at the wonder of the life developing inside me. This little one was a piece of myself, and I reflected on what kind of mother I would be, while keeping my thoughts to myself.

My heart had adjusted to this new reality: My pregnancy had flourished, despite my early desire to terminate it. With trepidation and courage, I resolved to do my best for this baby. I still wondered if I was making the right choice. With as much awareness as I could muster at the tender age of 20, I was hoping to develop the tools I would require as a mother.

A sudden surge of pain tightened across my belly. The pain took my breath away. *Braxton-Hicks contractions*, I thought, taking a deep breath and putting it out of my mind. I could feel the baby's feet pressing into my gallbladder, painful and sharp under my ribs. Suddenly excited, I marvelled at the prospect that soon this child would be delivered.

The contractions persisted intermittently for 24 hours before becoming regular, and with each one, the pain grew stronger, eventually accelerating from every 10 to every 5 minutes. At that point, my family decided it was time to make the one-hour drive to Lethbridge and check into the hospital.

We left home just after midnight, and my mom called my fiancé to inform him of our departure. Though I attempted to be brave, I was terrified inside. I kept my fear hidden, determined not to show it to anyone. Sitting in the back seat of my parent's car, I couldn't help but think my life was about to change forever.

Upon arrival at the hospital, I was officially admitted in labor. By 7:30 AM, progression had been slow, and the doctor decided to strip my membranes in hopes of speeding things up. Despite enduring another five hours of excruciating contractions that tightened my belly every 1-2 minutes, there was no effect.

After a total of nearly 46 hours of painful contractions, I was exhausted. Still, I failed to make progress. Contractions hit even harder, each one more agonizing. Finally, the doctor officially declared I had "failure to progress." *Failure? How often do I need to feel like this? I can't even do labour right!* I'd felt like a disappointing failure so much in the past year; deep inside, I knew I deserved this one, too. I had become a master at self-loathing and could add this to my list of screw-ups, one more thing to beat myself up about.

At 1 PM, preparations were made for surgery. Just as the anesthetist readied the epidural, my boyfriend walked into my hospital room but turned as white as a sheet and hastily left upon seeing the needle. Once again, I was alone with my thoughts as I was wheeled into the operating room for a cesarean section delivery.

It's difficult to describe the sensations that occurred behind the surgical drape. With the epidural in place, I was conscious throughout the entire procedure, wincing as the doctor pushed and pulled inside of me. The pressure in my abdomen was excruciating, and tears welled up in my eyes. As I pondered how my life was about to change, I felt a surge of release as the doctor held up a tiny, miraculous face over the operating drape.

"Congratulations, it's a boy!" the doctor exclaimed. Seeing him was surreal. *Is this my baby? Had I taken part in creating this miraculous being?*

Despite the miracle of my newborn son, I couldn't shake off the feeling of shame. My inability to progress in labor resulted in the surgical delivery of my baby, leaving me with a six-inch scar that served as a constant reminder of my shortcomings, failures, and disappointments.

As soon as I laid eyes on my son, all of my negative emotions dissipated, and I felt like I was witnessing a miracle. I was in complete awe of this little human being who had just entered the world. He was perfect in every way, from his delicate fingers to his bright eyes and light blond hair. It was as if my heart had grown ten times bigger, and I knew in that moment that I would do anything to protect him.

Holding him in my arms, I made a promise to myself that I would never abandon him, no matter what. His tiny hands wrapped around my finger, and I felt a love that I had never known before. It was a love that was pure and unconditional, and I knew that I would cherish it forever.

We had decided on the name Jonah during my pregnancy. However, after the excitement of the delivery day had settled and everyone had gone home, I found myself alone with my little one. As I held him, tracing his face with my finger and laying my hand on his tiny chest, I couldn't shake off the feeling that his name didn't quite fit. In the quiet of the night, I heard the name *Gabriel* whispered as a prayer in my ear. My heart skipped a beat - Gabriel, my angel. It was perfect.

Later, I asked my fiancé about the name, and he was just as shocked as I was. "That's weird," he responded, "I was just thinking the same thing!" We both laughed excitedly, eager to share the news of our new baby's name.

Baby Gabriel, a messenger of unconditional love and joy, had arrived.

As soon as I held Gabriel in my arms, I felt an overwhelming sense of love and connection. It was a love that I didn't know existed - deep, unconditional, and instantaneous. I was awed by this tiny human being that I had helped bring into the world. But, as much as I loved him, I also felt a sense of panic and uncertainty. I had never been a mother before, and the responsibility of caring for a newborn felt overwhelming.

Thankfully, I was blessed with an incredible support system. My family and close friends rallied around me, offering guidance, support, and love. They helped me navigate the sleepless nights, the endless feedings, and the many, many diaper changes. With their help, I was able to settle into my new role as a mother and begin to bond with my son.

Gabriel quickly became the center of our lives. He was such a gentle and joyful spirit, and his presence brought light and laughter into every room. His infectious smile and happy coos melted the hearts of everyone who met him. I was amazed at how such a small person could have such a big impact on the world around him.

Despite all the challenges I had faced in my past, holding Gabriel in my arms made me feel like everything was going to be okay. His snuggles and sweet baby scent were like a healing balm that soothed all my worries and fears. When I held him, I felt a sense of peace and purpose that I had never experienced before. I knew that I had been given a precious gift, and I was determined to cherish and protect it with all my heart.

As Gabriel grew, so did my responsibilities. Juggling nursing school and motherhood was challenging, but my parents stepped in to help. They welcomed Gabriel into their home on weekends so I could focus on my studies; watching him grow brought them immense joy. It was heartwarming to see the bond that developed between Gabriel and his grandparents.

But motherhood wasn't easy for me. Despite my love for Gabriel, I often felt overwhelmed and unsure of my abilities. Financial struggles added to the stress, and my husband had to make sacrifices to help care for our son. He left his job and began working at my parents' factory, so he could be closer to us.

Finding moments of peace and serenity in the midst of the chaos was rare but holding Gabriel in my arms made everything else fade away. We spent countless hours in the rocking chair, his tiny body nestled against mine. His contentment brought a sense of calm to my chaotic life. With each infant breath, I felt his sweet joy at life radiating through me.

As I held Gabriel close, the weight of responsibility and uncertainty weighed heavy on my heart. I knew that my upcoming marriage and motherhood would be a challenging journey, fraught with obstacles and unknowns. Yet, in the stillness of the night, I felt a stirring within my soul, a sense of purpose and belonging that transcended my fears and doubts. I realized that my life was not just a random sequence of events, but rather part of a greater plan orchestrated by a higher power. I was filled with gratitude for the blessings in my life, but also with humility in the face of the vast unknown that lay ahead.

Seeking guidance and solace beyond myself, I turned to prayer, surrendering myself to the wisdom and direction of the divine. I knew that the road ahead would be treacherous, but I had faith that I would be led and supported every step of the way. As I looked down at my sleeping child, I was struck by the miracle of life and the endless possibilities that awaited us. I was determined to embrace my journey with courage and trust, relying on the guidance and wisdom of the divine as I faced the joys and sorrows of motherhood and marriage.

On our wedding day, I stood in a white dress at the back of the church that felt unfamiliar and foreboding. The gravity of my decision and the magnitude of the commitment overwhelmed me. My doubts and fears whispered in my ear, making me question if this was truly part of God's plan for me. I felt like a caged bird, unable to spread my wings and chained to my past mistakes. My mind screamed that I wasn't ready for this commitment, and the pressure was too intense. Despite hoping my parents and fiancé would understand my emotions, I didn't have the courage to speak my truth. Reluctantly, I forced myself down the aisle, hiding my uncertainty and hoping for the best.

Later that night, I lay curled up in bed, facing the wall and praying with fervor. I felt trapped as if my wedding day was just another prison sentence, and I was now facing a life sentence. The weight of my doubts and fears bore down on me, threatening to crush my spirit. But in that moment of desperation, I felt a divine presence, a glimmer of hope and reassurance that I was not alone. I clung to that hope, surrendering myself to the wisdom and guidance of the divine, and found the strength to face the challenges ahead with renewed courage and faith.

Chapter Two

ANGEL GABRIEL

"I am Gabriel.
I stand in the very presence of God.
It was He who sent me to you..."

— *LUKE 1:19*

As Gabriel grew, so did his curiosity and sense of adventure. He loved exploring new places and trying new things, and I loved watching him discover the world around him. His sense of wonder and fearlessness were contagious, and I found myself embracing life with a renewed sense of joy and appreciation.

Despite the challenges we faced, Gabriel was a constant source of light and hope. He had an infectious energy that lifted everyone's spirits and reminded us of the beauty and magic of life. His mischievous streak only added to his charm, and I found myself laughing more than I had in years.

Watching Gabriel embrace his love of farming at my parents' sunflower farm was a particular joy. He was fascinated by every aspect of farming, from planting and harvesting to the intricacies of farm machinery. I loved watching him soak up the knowledge and wisdom of my parents and their farming community.

With each passing day, Gabriel grew more and more into his own person, with his own unique quirks and passions. I felt honored to be his mother, to guide him as he navigated the world and to watch him grow into the amazing person I knew he would become.

In the darkness of a cold November night, I awoke, gasping for breath, terrified and crying, every hair on my body standing up straight. In a dream, I had seen Gabriel's face, his beautiful, mischievous blue eyes wide and vacant. He was floating face up in the blue water of a swimming pool, his chest completely still. Gabriel had drowned.

It's just a bad dream, I breathlessly told myself. *Go back to sleep.*

Yet as I lay in bed, wide awake, my mind continued to race with shock — the dream felt so real! *Back to sleep?* I argued with myself. *Not a chance!*

Trembling, I rose out of bed. I tiptoed into Gabriel's room, placing my hand on his tiny chest as he slept. I traced his precious little cheek and kissed his forehead before retreating silently back to bed.

It's okay, Christy, I told myself. *Go back to sleep. Everything is right in your world.*

But for days, this dream of Gabriel haunted me, always there, in the back of my mind.

Driving home one night a month later, after picking up Gabriel from day care, a strange tension gnawed at me. I was annoyed at Gabriel's caregiver, who had just informed me that she could not watch Gabriel the following week as she was leaving town.

Going out of town? I thought. *It's my last week of university before Christmas break! I need to study! What will I do?*

Taking a breath to calm myself, I decided school would just have to wait. It was the holidays. Above all else, my heart's desire was to revel in the blessings of my life, especially the joy of having my beautiful boy by my side, and to cherish every moment spent with him.

Instead of studying, Gabriel and I went Christmas shopping. He was such a joy to be with! My perfect companion, we bustled from store to store, delighting in the Christmas decorations, songs and twinkling lights. We baked cookies and coloured pictures of Santa. Gabriel perched on the kitchen island, talking my ear off as I cooked dinner. At 29 months old, he was wise beyond his years. We had the best week ever.

And what better way to finish our perfect week than to visit Grandma and Grandpa at their farm! This was one of Gabriel's favourite places to be.

On our way to my parent's home, we stopped for family pictures to give them as Christmas gifts. Gabriel looked so handsome and grown-up in his blue denim shirt. His eyes sparkled with Christmas light, the photographer perfectly capturing his joyful essence amidst a studio backdrop of yellow flowers.

As we pulled up to the farm on that chilly December 6th evening, the air was filled with anticipation. My parents were waiting for us, eager to share their Christmas spirit. As soon as we caught a glimpse of the farm, Gabriel couldn't contain his excitement. He unhooked his seatbelt, stood up, and pumped his fists, shouting with glee, "Yes! Yes!"

My father had transformed the farm into a wonderland of twinkling Christmas lights. We led Gabriel into the living room while my father went outside to turn on the lights for the big reveal. Gabriel held his breath in suspense, and when the lights came on, his face lit up with astonishment and wonder.

"Pretty lights, Grandpa!!" he exclaimed in pure delight, his eyes shining brighter than any light on the farm.

The following morning was a bleak winter day, with temperatures below zero. I spent the day writing school papers while my parents played with Gabriel. They videotaped him as he strolled around the farm shops with my Dad and through the yard with my Mom, joyfully pointing out the glittering

Christmas lights. He played on the swing set and drove the forklift and truck with Grandpa, the two of them merrily cruising the neighbourhood.

By the end of that Saturday, Gabriel was exhausted. But something kept him from sleeping.

Against his typical easy-going nature, he shrieked so loud it chilled our bones. No one could settle Gabriel — not my husband, myself, or his beloved grandparents. *Why won't you just go to sleep?* my rattled brain pleaded as Gabriel's persistent cries pierced through the night. Frustrated and in tears, I yelled at him, "Gabriel, please go to sleep!" Instead, the crying went on.

And on.

And on.

We tried leaving him to self-soothe. That failed. We tried pulling him out of his bed to cuddle. For a moment, Gabriel would quiet and calm himself, but each time we placed him back in his bed, the wailing and shrieking would start all over again.

Finally, my heart could take no more. Entering his room, I was bewildered to find Gabriel standing in his bed, pointing somewhere behind me, yelling, "No, go away! Go away!"

Go away? Who was he talking to? Peering over my shoulder, I saw nothing — yet Gabriel adamantly warned this unseen character to go away. Whatever he saw terrified him. For the first time, he seemed frightened of the dark room.

Exhausted from screaming, he finally fell into what can only be described as a fitful sleep, often awakening that night, yelling and pointing at something imaginary. *"Go away!"* He clung to his dad and me in the middle of the night.

"Stay, Mom, stay!" he sobbed.

So we stayed, stroking his tear-streaked face and hugging Gabriel tight.

The following day was December 8, 2002. The air hung heavy with anticipation on that fateful December morning. Exhausted and cranky after Gabriel's nighttime theatrics, we decided to skip church and stay home.

After breakfast, Gabriel and his beloved new companion, Sullie, set out on a playful adventure. They frolicked and romped through the yard, the mischievous pup often knocking Gabriel over with his clumsy enthusiasm. We watched with joy, revelling in their youthful exuberance, but never thought to capture it on camera.

As we cleaned up the breakfast dishes, we suddenly spotted Gabriel perilously close to the busy highway. He had climbed the miniature Dutch windmill my parents had installed in the front yard, and my heart skipped a beat at the thought of what could have happened. My dad rushed out to bring him back to safety.

"Don't you dare go to the windmill without us again! It's dangerous near the road!" he admonished, fear and worry etched on his face.

As he pulled Gabriel away, he realized that he had accidentally broken a piece of the windmill. His eyes grew wide with sorrow as he looked up at my dad and pleaded, "Grandpa, fix it?"

With a tender smile, Papa promised to repair the damage.

Relieved now that Gabriel was safely home, I went to the farm office to finish writing my semester final nursing papers. Entering my last semester of University before graduating with my Bachelor of Nursing degree, I often found reprieve at my parent's farm, particularly on weekends. It allowed me time to complete my schoolwork while they enjoyed time with Gabriel.

Hours later, as I stepped outside the office, I heard my Dad yell from the far end of the farm, "There's no water here!"

Curious, I walked to the farm shop where my husband was repairing his truck. "Why is Papa looking for water?" I asked. My husband told me that Sullie had come running to the shop, soaking wet, but that Gabriel was nowhere around.

"I sent Gabriel to the house to get washed up for lunch a while ago," he said.

Confused, I stared at him. Suddenly my throat went dry: Gabriel had never reached the house.

A realization slammed into me. Heart pounding, I raced between my childhood home and the shop into our field. Half a mile across the field was our dugout, the farm's water supply. I was halfway there when I saw my Mom. She had rushed to the highway, remembering Gabriel's earlier excursion. From her vantage point, she could see Gabriel's little footsteps crunched into the snow, leading to the irrigation pond, where he'd followed the puppy. The farm pond, over twenty feet deep, had mostly frozen over, yet here Gabriel's footsteps led us until they eventually gave way and broke through the ice.

Panic crossed my mother's face, and she threw her arms in the air.

Immediately, I dropped to my knees, a sense of dread overcoming me. My whole body shook as I watched my husband sprint past me, scrambling as fast as he could through the snow to the pond, then launching himself into the icy water.

"Gabriel!!" I sobbed hysterically, tears streaming out too fast to wipe them. With a strength no longer my own, I rushed off to the dugout as my husband emerged from the ice, cradling Gabriel's limp body in his arms.

Gently he laid him on the grassy slope and started CPR. I knelt across from him to assist. My Dad arrived, out of breath, to see Gabriel's blue pants, red sweater, Velcro leather boots and blue coat were caked with ice. Instantly he dropped to his knees and took over CPR while my husband ran to the house to call 9-1-1.

"Breathe, Gabriel, breathe!!" I pleaded.

"Gabriel, come back!!" begged my Mom.

As our hysteria grew, I looked at Gabriel's blue face, shocked to see exactly the image I'd been stunned by months before in my dream. His vacant, glassy eyes told me the horrible truth. *He's gone*, I realized. *My baby!*

I cried with anguish and staggered to my feet, frozen in time, while my Dad continued CPR, pumping his tiny chest and praying to see a breath.

Finally, the ambulance arrived, and two EMTs rushed from the vehicle. "How long ago did you find him?" they asked. Mindlessly I somehow answered, watching them go to work. They cut away Gabriel's clothes and whisked him into the ambulance, pumping warm IV fluids through his veins as they sped off to the hospital.

Cold and shaking, we jumped in the family cars and followed. My husband was still in his work clothes, now soaking wet from his icy rescue, yet he refused dry clothes when the emergency room staff attempted to warm him up. There was nothing any of us needed — nothing except our little boy to pull through.

As the ER team worked feverishly to save Gabriel's life, we waited anxiously, hoping and praying for a miracle. Eventually, they decided to transfer him to a larger medical center, where a team of pediatricians awaited. They were in constant contact with a leading trauma physician in Calgary, who guided them through the necessary steps to revive our baby boy.

Word of Gabriel's condition spread quickly, and soon our friends, family, and clergy had all gathered in the waiting room. We clung to each other, alternating between tears, prayer, and desperate hope as the emergency team fought to keep Gabriel alive.

Six agonizing hours crawled by before the doctor finally emerged from the room. Her eyes were red with tears, and her voice cracked as she delivered the news we feared the most.

"There is nothing more we can do," she said, her head bowed in sorrow.

I let out a gutteral scream, unable to bear the thought of losing my son.

The doctors and nurses began to disconnect the tubes and machines that had been keeping Gabriel alive.

As the nurse placed Gabriel in my arms for the last time, I cradled him gently, knowing that he was slipping away from me forever. My world crumbled around me, and time seemed to stand still as I said my final good-byes to my beloved child.

I looked at his face in wonder again as I traced it with my finger, etching it into my heart, memorizing every feature, every freckle. I kissed his lips, cheeks, and eyes, holding him close to my heart. I prayed for a miracle. This could not be real.

I wanted to hold him in my arms forever — yet I knew everyone needed their chance to say goodbye. Gabriel was passed from my arms to my husband, parents, and his nana. Then to any aunts, uncles, and friends who wanted one last chance to hold him.

As shock and denial continued to pound my thoughts, the nurses took Gabriel's hand and footprints and snipped a piece of his hair to give us, along with a stuffed angel toy, a keepsake to fill our empty arms and shattered hearts.

Driving home from the hospital, the weight of our grief was suffocating. Gabriel's red sweater and blue pants, cut off by the EMTs, lay between my husband and me, a constant reminder of what we had lost. The events of the day had left us speechless, and we were left to navigate a future that we never imagined.

The next day, the weight of grief hung heavy as friends and family visited. I mechanically served them coffee and meals, trying to act normal while my heart was shattered into a million pieces. The condolences and hugs were appreciated, but nothing could ease the pain of losing my precious Gabriel. I felt like a performer, putting on a brave face for the world when all I wanted to do was scream and cry.

The drive to the funeral home felt like an eternity. Each passing minute was like a stab in the heart, a reminder of what we were about to face. The pit in my stomach grew with each mile, and my hands shook as I clung to the steering wheel. Finally, we arrived, and I felt a sense of dread wash over me as we stepped into the building.

The funeral home was a blur as the director led us to where Gabriel lay, his little body covered in a yellow-striped pediatric gown. My heart stopped as I saw him lying there, so still and cold on the stainless-steel table. The reality of our loss hit me like a ton of bricks, and I felt like I couldn't breathe. Every step towards him was like walking through quicksand, and every moment spent with him was both excruciating and sacred.

The funeral director offered to dress Gabriel, but my husband and I knew we had to do it ourselves. I couldn't bear the thought of strangers dressing him for his final goodbye. As I buttoned his shirt and smoothed his hair, memories flooded my mind. The pain of loss was unbearable, and the tears flowed freely.

The reality of never dressing him or brushing his hair again devastated me. I would never feel the warmth of his lips or hear his sweet voice again. It was all gone, and my heart felt like it would never be whole again.

As we prepared our little boy for his final farewell, a divine moment enveloped us. The presence of the Holy Spirit filled the room, washing over us in waves. We were in a sacred space, separate from the world outside. With each button we fastened, we felt the weight of our grief, but also a sense of peace. The Holy Spirit was with us, guiding us through this painful moment. As I wiped the tear leaking from the corner of Gabriel's eye, I felt a connection to him that transcended life and death. His tears matched my own, and I knew that we were forever linked, even though he was no longer with me. It was a reminder that his spirit lived on, and that he would always be a part of us. But the thought of never seeing his smiling face or hearing his voice again was almost too much to bear.

The enormity of the loss was overwhelming, and I wondered how I would ever fill the void that Gabriel had left behind.

Recovering from tragedy and loss is a journey of the soul, one that is fraught with obstacles and challenges that test our very being. It is a path that can take years to traverse, and one that requires us to confront our deepest fears and emotions.

In the wake of loss, we are often consumed by numbness and shock, unable to comprehend the enormity of our pain. And yet, as time passes, we are forced to confront the reality of our situation, as the rollercoaster of emotional turbulence begins to take hold.

Anniversaries, birthdays, and holidays become charged with mystery, as we wonder what each day will bring. Sometimes, we are knocked off our feet by grief, while other times we are filled with a quiet calm. And through it all, we learn to move with the ebb and flow of our emotions, allowing ourselves to be exactly as we are, without judgment or expectation.

For there is no timeline for grief, no set path that we must follow. It can strike us in the most unexpected of moments, even in moments of joy. And yet, it is important that we allow ourselves to feel these emotions fully, surrendering to the pain and allowing ourselves to move through them without getting stuck.

In our current lives, we often do not take adequate time to grieve. We immediately go back to work and make ourselves busy, pushing those darker emotions of grief away. But the truth is, there is no greater gift we can give ourselves than the time and space to feel our emotions fully, energetically, physically, and spiritually.

For not processing these emotions properly can lead to physical issues, as the dense energy of grief becomes stuck in our energetic field. And it can also lead to feelings of separation and abandonment, making the grief journey even more isolating.

As time passes, those around us who are not at the heart of the loss tend to move on with their own lives. And suddenly, we find ourselves alone, without the cocoon of support that once surrounded us. But even in these dark days, there is hope, as we find the same life force energy that helped us get out of bed, shower, and make dinner for our families.

For me, two things pulled me through those days of intense grief: my journal and my faith. Through my journal, I was able to express the depth of my emotions in a way that was raw and unfiltered. And through my faith, I was able to find a power greater than myself, one that helped me navigate the darkest of days.

And as I look back on those journal entries today, I am reminded of the darkness of those days, but also of the light that shone amidst the dark.

For even in our darkest moments, there is always hope, always a glimmer of light that can guide us through the pain and towards healing.

Chapter Three

THE VOID

The analyst must go on learning endlessly…
It is his own hurt that gives the measure of his power to heal.
This, and nothing else,
is the meaning of the Greek myth of the wounded physician.

~ Carl Jung

All over the world, tragedies occur every single moment of every single day. There is nothing special about my circumstances and grief.

Loss is universal.

Multitudes of people throughout the globe are experiencing the aftershock of tragedy and loss at any given moment. Humans cry out in pain in their suffering, unsure where to turn.

Navigating the depths of grief is a daunting task, one that can feel like being lost in an infinite, dark sea without a compass. The weight of sorrow can feel like a heavy cloak, suffocating and overwhelming. Yet, some find their way through the darkness, inching towards a glimmer of light that grows brighter with each step. It is a journey that leaves scars, but also imbues those who make it through with a strength born of resilience and hard-won wisdom.

For some, the path through grief is never found, and the pain of loss remains a constant companion. But for those who emerge from the darkness, there is often a newfound sense of purpose. They become wounded healers, using their experience to help others navigate their own emotional struggles. In this way, the pain they once carried becomes a source of strength and hope, a beacon of light in the darkness for those still struggling to find their way.

The aftermath of Gabriel's funeral was a blur of overwhelming emotions that I couldn't even begin to process. It felt like time had slowed to a crawl as I struggled to accept the unbearable reality that my precious child was gone forever. Our once bustling farmhouse was now a hauntingly empty shell of its former self. The silence was deafening, and the void left by Gabriel's absence felt suffocating. The only solace I could find was cherishing every touch and every memory of him.

As the holidays approached, I was consumed by a deep sense of sorrow and loss. The Christmas gifts that Gabriel and I had picked out together lay unopened and unwrapped under the tree, mocking me with their glittering presence. Every festive decoration, every carol, and every family gathering, only served as a constant reminder of the irreplaceable emptiness in my heart. As the world rejoiced in the miracle of God's Son, I felt abandoned and alone, lost in the depths of my own grief.

It wasn't until three days after Christmas when I could no longer bear the weight of my sorrow, that I found a way to release the flood of emotions that had been building inside me. With shaking hands and tears streaming down my face, I opened my journal and began pouring out my heart to my sweet little angel in Heaven. Each word was a cry of pain, a desperate plea for comfort and understanding. But as I wrote, a glimmer of hope began to emerge from the darkness. And in that moment, I realized that even in my deepest despair, I was never truly alone.

December 28, 2002

Dear Gabriel,

As I sit here 20 days after our whole world changed, I miss you. I am angry you are gone from us. I am saddened by the void, the empty space in my life. I feel like I'm suffocating and can't gasp for air. I'm having such a difficult time trying to understand why this tragedy happened.

I long for your sweet "Eskimo" kisses and muddy boots running in the living room. I miss your dirty fingerprints on the windows and walls. I miss your winks and your smiles. I miss your sweet "Night, night Mom, I love you Mom!" I keep hoping to see your bed ruffled and anticipate your quick footsteps first thing in the morning...

I would give anything just to hold you in my arms again. My heart aches for you. Please watch over us. I love you.

Surviving that first Christmas was nothing short of a miracle. My heart was heavy, burdened by an unbearable weight. It felt as if there was a gaping void in our home, in our family, and within myself. Anger consumed me, a fiery rage that burned deep within my soul. How could I not hold my precious Gabriel, hug him, and tell him how much he meant to me? I was livid at God for taking him away. *Why did it have to be my sweet, innocent Gabriel? Wasn't the love we had for him enough? Didn't we need him?*

The storm of emotions within me was building, and I was terrified of what would happen when it finally broke free. So I pushed it down, burying it deep beneath the surface. To the outside world, I appeared strong, a pillar of resilience. But beneath that facade, I was numb, frozen in place. Each day was a struggle to keep going, to keep moving forward in a life that no longer held any meaning. There was no hope, no joy, no future to look forward to.

But there were moments when reality hit me like a ton of bricks. I would walk to the water where Gabriel's life was tragically taken away. The memory of his tiny footprints on the ice haunted me, leading me to the spot where the ice gave way and swallowed him whole. And then one day, I found his ski cap floating in the water, a silent witness to the horror that had befallen my precious child. I dropped to my knees, my heart wrenching in agony. I screamed my pain and my fury at God, begging Him to explain why He had taken my Gabriel away. At times, the depth of my despair seemed bottomless, and I couldn't accept that this nightmare was my new reality.

I sat across from my manager, my heart heavy with grief, my eyes swollen and red from crying. The pain of losing Gabriel was still raw and fresh, and I had just received news of another tragic loss. Our 16-year-old neighbor, whom I had babysat for years, had passed away in a car accident. My heart shattered into a million pieces once again, as it had only been a few months since our own family tragedy.

I grew up in a tight-knit rural farming community, where tragedy had struck twice before. My best friend's mom had passed away unexpectedly from a brain tumor thirteen months to the day before Gabriel. And now, just months after Gabriel's death, we were collectively reeling in the wake of another loss. The pain and suffering seemed never-ending.

Sitting in my manager's office, I was an emotional mess. I needed some time to gather myself and come to terms with this new wave of grief, but instead of the support and understanding I had hoped for, I was met with a callous response. "You're just going to have to get over it, Christy!" My manager's words hit me like a slap in the face. I was appalled and shocked. Clearly, this woman had never experienced the depths of grief before.

But the truth is, you don't just "get over it." Grief is messy and unpredictable. It hits unexpectedly and can be triggered by the smallest things. Even now, twenty years later, tidal waves of grief still wash over me, often catching me by surprise. But with time, I have learned to navigate these waters more gracefully. I have learned to give myself the space and time I need to grieve, and I have learned that healing is a slow and ongoing process.

In the depths of my despair, one night, I found myself trapped in a nightmare. It wasn't just any dream, it was a vivid representation of my own reality. As I lay there sleeping, I felt the coldness of a needle piercing through my skin, and a foreign substance slowly entering my veins. It paralyzed me from the inside out, leaving me unable to move or speak. I was screaming out for someone, anyone, to hear my silent cries for help. But no one came.

That dream was a haunting reflection of my true inner self. I was suffocating under the weight of my grief, feeling lost and alone in a world that didn't understand me. It seemed like everyone around me was going about their day-to-day lives, oblivious to the hurricane raging within me. I put on a brave face, trying to convince myself and others that I was fine. But the truth was, I was barely holding on.

All I wanted was for someone to see past my facade, to notice the pain etched onto my face and reach out to help. But time and time again, my hopes were dashed. No one seemed to grasp the extent of my suffering, leaving me feeling isolated and abandoned.

When you experience significant loss or trauma, it can feel like you're being swept up in a powerful emotional storm. There are several different models, or frameworks that may assist in understanding grief. While I can find similarites in all of the models, one that resonated deeply with my own experience of traversing the ebb and flow of grief is The Dual Process of Coping with Bereavement, as proposed by Margaret Stroebe and Henk Schut. This model acknowledges that individuals grieving a loss oscillate between two primary coping processes: loss-oriented coping and restoration-oriented coping.

In my grief journey, I found myself engaging in loss-oriented coping, which involved facing the raw emotional pain, sorrow, and grief associated with the loss. It allowed me the space to confront the reality of the loss, to express my emotions freely, and to participate in activities that honored the memory of my loved one. This process gave me permission to fully embrace my grief and take the necessary steps to heal.

Simultaneously, I also experienced restoration-oriented coping, focusing on the practical and functional changes that resulted from the loss. It meant adapting to a new life without my loved ones, establishing new routines, and seeking to find meaning and purpose beyond my grief. This aspect of coping helped me rebuild my life and navigate the challenges of moving forward, while still honoring the significance of myloss.

Understanding the coexistence and interaction of these two coping processes was crucial for me. It allowed me to give myself permission to grieve and mourn while also seeking ways to rebuild and find balance and purpose in my life. I realized that it was not a matter of choosing one over the other, but rather embracing both aspects as integral parts of my healing journey.

I came to understand that grief is a deeply personal experience, and no two individuals will grieve in the same way. It is a unique and individual process that requires allowing oneself to go through it in one's own way, without judgment or comparison.

Ultimately, the Dual Process of Coping with Bereavement served as a guiding light in my journey of healing. It helped me navigate the complexities of grief, acknowledge the pain of the loss, and embrace the possibilities of restoration and growth. By honoring both aspects of coping, I have been able to integrate my loss into my life, finding a way to move forward while keeping the memory of my loved one alive.

Loss can leave us feeling abandoned and lost in a sea of confusion, but even in the darkest moments, I've felt a glimmer of faith holding me up. I may never understand why I had to experience this pain, but I know that losing someone as dear as Gabriel was part of a bigger plan, one beyond my comprehension. However, that doesn't mean I haven't felt betrayed by the universe and lashed out at God.

The truth is, grief demands the expression of our most intense emotions; otherwise, we risk getting lost in them forever.

Losing a child is a devastating experience that can have a profound impact on a marriage. There's no handbook on how to navigate such a loss, and it can feel like a rupture in the natural order of life. As a parent who has gone through this traumatic event, I have experienced a range of intense emotions, such as anger, sadness, and despair. These emotions can lead to tension and strain in a relationship, causing breakdowns in communication. In my case, my spouse and I struggled to find the right words to express our feelings, and we avoided discussing our loss altogether. This led to further distance and tension between us.

Blame and resentment can also arise as we each try to cope with the loss in our own way, feeling like our partner is not providing enough support. We may have different ways of grieving, leading to misunderstandings and conflict. Loss takes a toll on physical and emotional intimacy, making it difficult to feel close and connected.

The loss of a loved one can shatter our world, leaving us feeling alone and adrift in a sea of grief. The emptiness and void can be overwhelming, causing a flood of emotions that we struggle to contain. The sadness and despair can be all-consuming, making it difficult to focus on even the simplest of tasks. We go through the motions of daily life, but time passes without any real meaning or purpose. Everything feels different, as if the ground beneath us has shifted and we're left struggling to find our footing. We're forced to confront a new reality, one that we never could have imagined, and the prospect of finding a "new normal" seems impossible. The weight of the loss is crushing, and the road ahead feels uncertain and terrifying.

As I stood in front of the mirror, my heart heavy with grief, I struggled to make sense of the conflicting emotions coursing through me. It had been just five months since I had lost Gabriel, and now I found myself pregnant again. The thought of bringing another child into the world filled me with both joy and terror.

I worried endlessly about the toll my fragile emotional state would have on the new life growing within me. *Could I be the mother this child needed, when I was still struggling to come to terms with the loss of my first-born? Would I ever be able to love again, knowing how quickly that love could be snatched away?*

The answers eluded me, and I found myself overwhelmed by sadness and despair. But then, a glimmer of hope appeared. My daughter, Micah, was born via planned cesarean section, and as I held her in my arms, I felt a deep sense of joy and love that was all the more profound for the pain that had come before. Holding Micah was a bittersweet reminder of what I had gone through and what I had lost. But at the same time, it also felt like a sign of hope and resilience. I knew that while I could never replace Gabriel, I could still find joy and love in my life, and Micah was a testament to that. She was a reminder that life goes on, even in the face of tragedy, and that there can be moments of beauty and happiness even in the darkest of times.

In that moment, I realized that the human experience is a complex tapestry of emotions, woven from joy and sorrow, love and loss. It is in the face of tragedy that we are forced to confront the deepest questions of existence, to find meaning in the midst of pain.

For me, that meant finding the strength to carry on, to love again, and to hold onto hope for the future. It meant accepting the fragility and beauty of life, and finding a way to navigate the complex emotions that come with loss. And it meant embracing the joy and love that can still be found, even in the midst of grief.

The loss of a loved one is a profound and transformative experience that can shake us to the core. It forces us to confront the impermanence and fragility of life, and challenges our understanding of who we are and what we value. In the aftermath of such a loss, we may find ourselves adrift, struggling to find our footing and make sense of the world around us.

Yet even in the midst of this turmoil, there is hope. We can draw strength and support from those around us, and from the depths of our own resilience. We may find that we are capable of more than we ever imagined, of overcoming seemingly insurmountable obstacles and finding a new sense of purpose and meaning.

The process of grieving is a complex and multifaceted one, encompassing a wide range of emotions and experiences. But we must remember that grief is not something to be feared or avoided, but rather something to be embraced and accepted as an integral part of the human experience. In doing so, we can find the strength to navigate the waters of loss and emerge on the other side with a renewed sense of hope and resilience.

As I walked through the aisles of Walmart two years after Gabriel's death, I couldn't help but feel a sense of emptiness. Suddenly, I heard a little boy around Gabriel's age throwing a tantrum, and memories of my own son flooded my mind. I smiled at the thought of taking those moments for granted, only to be shaken to my core as I heard the boy's mother call out, "Gabriel!! Come back here right NOW!" It was as if time stood still, and I was frozen in place as grief took over like a tornado, tearing down any sense of normalcy. My basket slipped from my fingers as I stumbled out of the store, my body wracked with sobs that seemed to come from the very depths of my being.

In the same time frame, I was pregnant with my second daughter, but it was bittersweet. For we were still residing in the same house that Gabriel had called home. His room remained untouched, a pristine monument to his memory. But the reality was that we couldn't keep his room forever, frozen in time as a time capsule of the past. It was a sacred space for me, a place where I could sit in his rocking chair surrounded by his toys and stuffed animals and feel close to him. But the thought of packing up his belongings and using his room for another child felt like an unbearable betrayal. It was an insurmountable task that I knew I couldn't avoid any longer.

As I began the process of sorting through his things, memories of Gabriel flooded me like a storm surge. I sat on his toddler bed, tears streaming down my face, clinging to his clothes, hoping to catch a whiff of his scent. I knew that we couldn't remain in the same house forever, not with his room as it was. And so, we began the search for our new family home.

The task of deciding what to keep and what to give away was almost too much to bear. Every item felt like a piece of him, and the thought of letting go was almost too much to bear. But with painstaking care, I sorted through his belongings, preparing his clothes to give away, deciding which stuffed animals to give to his sisters, and which ones were just too painful to part with.

As I sit here today, I can still feel the weight of that grief. It was the first of many purges of the only earthly reminder of his existence, and with each one, it felt like I was letting go of a piece of him all over again.

Shortly after moving into our new family home, at 31 weeks pregnant, I was admitted to the hospital in pre-term labor. *It's too early!* As I lay in the hospital bed, fear and worry consumed me. I prayed to God, begging Him not to take my precious child away from me.

Miraculously, my prayers were answered. Annika was born, at 37 weeks via cesarean section, three weeks early, but perfect in every way.

As I held my newborn daughter in my arms, tears of joy streamed down my face as I marveled at her perfect features. It was as if Gabriel's essence had been infused into her being. She was gorgeous with blue eyes and blond hair. This precious gift from God, who had answered my prayers for her safe arrival, brought immense comfort to my soul. And as I watched Micah eagerly and protectively dote on her little sister, I felt a deep sense of gratitude for the family that God had blessed me with. The love that filled our home was a reminder that, even in times of uncertainty and fear, there is always hope and goodness to be found.

As I sat holding my daughters, I couldn't help but reflect on the journey that had led me to this moment. In the midst of my fear and uncertainty, God had taken my anger and replaced it with peace. He had shown me mercy and covered my pain in a way that only He could.

It was a humbling realization, one that made me feel both grateful and awed by the power of the Divine. As tears of gratitude streamed down my face, I knew that I would never forget this moment and the profound sense of connection it brought.

Chapter Four

THE LIGHT ETERNAL

M y career as a nurse and the unconditional love of my daughters brought me a sense of purpose and normalcy. Despite the struggles my husband and I faced in expressing our grief, we remained steadfast in supporting one another, refusing to succumb to the heartbreaking statistics of a marriage ending after the loss of a child.

However, just as I felt secure in my life, a new obstacle emerged, threatening to shatter my hard-earned stability. As I stared down the possibility of yet another devastating loss, I was forced to dig deep and confront my inner reserves of strength and resilience.

"No one dies from this," my Mom said as she stared out my kitchen window.

It was December 7, 2006. Tomorrow will be the fourth anniversary of our family tragedy—four years since the death of my beautiful Gabriel.

Standing by my kitchen island drying dishes, I stared incredulously, her words sinking in. Closing my eyes, I took a deep breath. *Endometrial cancer,* I thought. *This can't be!*

As a nurse, I knew her diagnosis meant an uphill battle. Personally, I was terrified at the thought of losing my mom, so close on the heels of losing my son. My mind immediately played the worst-case scenarios. Previous trauma has conditioned us to believe the worst outcome in any situation.

"Actually," I replied, months of fear and anger bubbling out, "a nurse at my office just died from this, Mom." I was furious with her! For months she had ignored her physical symptoms, including abnormal bleeding. Was she in denial? Had she heard the doctor's diagnosis earlier that day and decided to ignore it?

As Mom drove home that night, I spent hours in contemplation, then turned to the one place I always found peace from my worst fears and refuge from my sorrow.

My journal.

December 8, 2006

Hello, my baby boy. Incredibly, we have now survived four years without you. This past year was the most difficult. I can't seem to find the happiness I once had. I lost it when we lost you. I buried a massive part of myself with you, and I just can't seem to surface. People tell me, "You're so strong…" but I don't feel strong. I feel broken. I can't count the times I've cried myself to sleep.

Grandma was diagnosed with cancer yesterday. I pray you watch over us all and help our hearts and Grandma's body mend.

The next few days were a nonstop frenzy. Negative thoughts swirled in my head. I told myself I shouldn't dwell on the worst-case scenarios. Yet I couldn't help but picture my parents' emotional struggle. In addition to coping with Gabriel's loss, they were dealing with a fast-growing family business and were now facing a significant health crisis. How would they handle all this stress?

On the other hand, I faced a challenge, struggling to balance helping my parents and being in the way. I was a busy young mom with two toddler daughters, a part-time job and a marriage to keep together. Yet my fear of losing another loved one haunted me each day.

In January of 2007, Mom was referred to a cancer treatment center in Calgary. She underwent a hysterectomy, and her doctors held out hope that the cancer had not spread beyond her uterus.

A week later, while recovering from surgery, she received an urgent call from her surgeon. Results detected cancer cells in the surgical wash, and chemotherapy was recommended.

Hearing this news, our world caved in. *How could this be happening?* Mom lived an incredibly healthy lifestyle, and she and Papa walked miles religiously every day, rain or sunshine. Rarely did she eat sugar, and she maintained a well-balanced nutritious diet.

In addition, she was a believer in alternative therapy. Instead of following the doctor's recommendations, she explored unconventional nutritional and juicing options. Mom cut all red meat, dairy, eggs, and soy from her diet and she drank only fresh-pressed fruit and vegetable juices. For a few months, she experienced positive results and seemed vibrant. She became a biofeedback practitioner and continued her path of complementary therapies to find a cure for the free-floating cancer cells that remained outside the margins of the tumour.

For weeks, then months, all was well. There was no further bad news. Mom was fighting this beast and winning.

My parents hosted an employee Christmas party in Calgary a year after the surgery. As they walked into the party, Mom slipped on the ice and fell, breaking her wrist. An ordinary chance occurrence, she explained, yet my intuitions of doom told me otherwise.

The cancer is back, I thought to myself. Mom's intense resistance met my intuitive urge for her to return to the doctor. I prayed I wasn't coming from a place of fear but of care and compassion. However, a few weeks later, we could no longer ignore the signs.

Meeting her physician, she learned the awful truth: the cancer had returned, growing where her uterus had once been, and was now attached to her bladder. Her surgeon recommended performing complete pelvic cleaning surgery and subsequent treatment options.

Mom, Papa and I looked at each other in shock. *A year in the hospital battling infections and post-op complications? If she survived? Then further complications from chemotherapy? What choice is there?* Mom stared at the doctor, obviously not expecting this radical course of action.

Visibly upset, she snapped at the doctor, "I wouldn't treat my dog that way."

The doctor barely choked out another word. Later, amidst criticism from her friends and family, Papa and I would stand alongside my mother's choice. Though we sometimes struggled to understand her reasons, somehow we both knew our unconditional support and love would serve her best. That didn't make it any easier, though. This became an exercise in which my dad and I would learn to hold space. Holding space for someone means supporting someone without bias or judgment.

Through my mom's journey, I learned her best fighting chance was following the path she had faith in. It wasn't easy to set our own judgements and biases aside; however, we quickly realized that my mom only needed our unconditional support.

Over the next three years, she sought alternative treatments throughout North America with my father at her side. She was determined to fight this—her way.

She attended biofeedback courses in Puerto Vallarta, received stem cell therapy in Tijuana, and had hyperthermia and radiation in Los Angeles. Back in Calgary, she went in for Vitamin C infusions and another concoction of vitamins and minerals. While gagging, she choked down mushroom liquid extractions. Mom received mistletoe and Vitamin B17 injections. She tightened an already-strict diet. She practiced meditation and sound therapy and even tried baking soda therapy, attempting to make her body more alkaline. All in an attempt to eliminate the cancer cells.

As I watched my mother suffer through agonizing abdominal and pelvic pain, I felt helpless and overwhelmed. Even with the help of opioid medication, she still struggled to find relief. Tears streamed down her face as she tried to soothe herself, and I wished I could do more to ease her suffering.

But my mom was a fighter, and she refused to give up in the face of such pain. For three long years, we stood by her side, watching and waiting as she battled through each day. She was a warrior, determined to overcome her illness no matter what the cost.

Through it all, we prayed for her recovery, hoping that one day she would be free from the pain that had plagued her for so long. And despite the challenges and setbacks, my mother never lost hope, inspiring us all to keep fighting alongside her.

The devastating blows continued. Seeing the bleakness of her health situation, she reluctantly agreed to begin low-dose chemotherapy. Immediately the side effects manifested; extreme nausea and hair loss.

Sensitive to her ill appearance, Mom refused to cover her head with a scarf. Grudgingly, we drove to the appointment for a wig fitting. As the compassionate hairdresser shaved what little remained of Mom's beautiful grey locks, I knelt before her, holding her tight while she sobbed like a little girl. All along, I'd promised we'd fight this together. Now I wanted to cradle her on my lap and tell her everything would be okay, as she had done for me a thousand times. Watching each lock of hair flutter to the floor while my Mom sobbed intensely, it took every morsel of self-restraint not to break down and cry alongside her.

The next few months were a rollercoaster of emotions. My attention was divided between my mother's health and the needs of my young family, leaving me feeling torn and trapped. With my daughters in pre-kindergarten and primary school, I was constantly pulled in multiple directions. I had commitments to volunteer in their classrooms and lead fundraising efforts for the parent's association. On top of that, my nursing job demanded my attention. Meanwhile, my husband worked long hours at a factory and had a two-hour commute each day. I scrambled to find childcare so I could travel to Calgary to support my Mom's care, feeling like this was where I was needed the most. But this left my marriage under immense pressure. I was overwhelmed with a sense of duty and responsibility towards everyone, leaving no time or energy to care for myself.

One day from my room at my parent's home, I heard muffled cries echoing off the walls. As I approached the bathroom upstairs, my heart sank as I recognized the sound of my mother's tears. I inched closer, my hand shaking as I reached for the door handle. Inside, my mother sat slumped in the bathtub, her body trembling with sobs. I couldn't bear to see her like this.

"Mom? Are you okay?" I whispered, my voice barely audible over her cries.

She shook her head, her eyes squeezed shut as she clutched her chest. "I can't get out of the tub," she moaned, her bony fingers tracing the outline of her ribcage.

My heart ached as I saw her frail and fragile body. I stepped forward, gently stroking her back, trying to offer any comfort I could. Her skin was so thin and papery beneath my touch. I wrapped my arms around her, holding her close as I lifted her from the tub. She was a mere shadow of the strong and vibrant woman I knew, her six-foot frame now weighing in at a mere 125 pounds.

Seeing her in this vulnerable state shattered me. The fierce light of faith in her eyes had dimmed, and for the first time, I saw a flicker of defeat. But my mom was a fighter, and she never lost the will to keep pushing forward.

A few weeks later, in early April, I awaited my parents' arrival at the Calgary airport as they journeyed home from Mom's latest treatment in Mexico. My heart sank as I watched my once strong and resilient mother being wheeled out in a wheelchair, her eyes hollow, and her spirit crushed. I couldn't bear to imagine what she had been through. This last surgery had been arduous, taking every ounce of her strength to withstand.

Though I attempted to hide my shock, I realized as we drove in silence my Mom was no longer the same woman I had left weeks earlier.

Papa and I helped lift her into the car. Squeezing my eyes shut against stinging tears, I feared losing another family member slamming me all over again.

As Mom settled in at home, there was a shift in the family dynamic. The air was tense, and Mom continued to be withdrawn and quiet. The Palliative Care physician frequently visited during this time, and home care nurses arrived daily. There was some confusion about whether Mom was recuperating from surgery or nearing the end of life. While her lab values continued to improve, she showed signs of withering away, withdrawing from Papa and me.

Bit by bit, I witnessed my strong mother slip away. Now I rarely saw my own young family. On weekends, my husband brought the girls to my parent's home so I could spend time with them. The girls didn't understand why Grandma couldn't play with them and why she wouldn't get out of bed. It broke my heart to watch these beautiful children—girls who had once brought Mom so much delight—no longer able to elicit a response from her. Mom had grown so tired, and as much as she tried, she simply had nothing left to give.

Each day, I spent hours lying beside her, holding her hand while she slept. At night, I listened from my bed downstairs for the scrape of her feet shuffling across the floor as she stumbled to the bathroom. Caring for her was like caring for a newborn. I never relaxed into a deep sleep, carefully attuned to listening for any sign my help was needed, for relief from the pain, mercy, and radical healing.

One afternoon she rallied and sat up in bed, talking, which we had not heard in a week. I laid my head on her lap. She rubbed my cheek as she had done my entire life and said, "You're my best girl. You did it all." I sobbed; I was so far from having done it all, but what I had done had been with great love for her.

In retrospect, I didn't realize this would be our last meaningful conversation, the last time I heard Mom call me her best girl. It reminded me of the countless times she tucked me into bed as a child, caressing my tiny cheek and kissing my forehead while she repeated that tender phrase. Clinging to Mom's embrace returned me to that feeling of protection, security, and safety.

Later that week, my Dad and I discussed Mom's care. "If we could just get more food into her, she'd become stronger and bounce back!" Papa implored.

"It would do more harm to force her to eat, Papa," I replied. He looked at me incredulously. "So, I'm just supposed to give up on her?" he asked.

With tears, I answered, "There's a big difference between giving up and letting go."

For weeks the words had been bubbling inside me. We had to accept the inevitability of her fate and find a way to make her remaining days as peaceful and comfortable as possible. It was a difficult and painful decision, but it was one that we had to make if we wanted to honor her life and legacy.

During her final weeks, Mom claimed a donkey kept coming to visit her. "A donkey?" I asked, trying to pretend everything was fine. Mom persisted: "And he keeps telling me, 'All things come in perfect timing.'" When our priest visited, I talked to him about these strange visions. He explained she was hallucinating and that it was the medication. Yet I sensed something far more profound than medication-induced hallucinations. Mom had also been experiencing visitations from several of her departed loved ones.

A few days later, she told me she'd been speaking with her brothers when in reality, no one else was in the room. She didn't realize those brothers had passed away years before.

Is there something happening beyond my understanding? I wondered. *Is there more to this process of transitioning than just a physical death? Is Mom experiencing a reality beyond the veil?*

Overnight, there had been a startling change in Mom's condition. Her eyes were partially open and fixed, and she was no longer responsive, her breathing laboured. *She's had a stroke,* I thought.

I called the palliative care team. The doctor ordered medications administered subcutaneously; she could no longer swallow pills. Included was a medicine to settle her should she become agitated, as patients often do as they draw into their final hours of life.

The hours ticked by. I felt helpless. I closed my eyes, soaking in the love I felt for my Mom. I knew the final day would soon come, and Mom was going Home.

As family and visitors arrived to see Mom, I quietly lay on her bed, praying to let her go gracefully. I counted each second between her breaths, terrified for the moment I would hear the last one. As her breaths laboured, I refused to leave her side. Innately sensing her imminent transition, I felt a calm surrender, and my father moved to clear the room of visitors.

Mom had not spoken all day. I laid my head on her stomach and caught her eye. Suddenly, she jolted and blurted out, "Oh, hi!" I was confused; she wasn't speaking to me but to a spot on the wall.

My pulse quickened. "Is Gabriel here, Mom?" I asked.

Mom nodded and slowly pointed her finger at that same spot on the wall.

"Then go to him," I whispered, reassuring her. "We will be okay. I promise. We love you."

Nodding, she closed her eyes, breathing in and out slowly.

Just then, my Dad entered. Quietly I asked him to sit with us, opposite me, holding Mom's other hand. Hearing the gurgle and wheeze of her lungs, he looked at me with alarm. "I don't know if I can do this," he said.

With a calm strength I had never experienced, I reassured my father. "We'll do this together."

Papa cleared his throat, trying to stem the tide of tears that would soon pour out. Immediately, Mom's breathing became more laboured. I gripped her hand as she drew her last breath, our hearts in communion as she transitioned from this life to the great beyond. The comforting presence of the Light Eternal enveloped us, erasing all fear.

As her breathing ceased, a holy hush entered my soul. The room fell silent. This was her ultimate gift to me: A final tear escaped her left eye. As I wiped it from her cheek, I let out a sigh of relief. *Your suffering is finally over!* My father and I clasped hands, both of us trembling, bound in spirit. An enormous weight lifted from our shoulders. The burden of her care had been long and arduous; now, it was over. Suddenly overcome with sorrow, we broke out in sobs.

She's no longer here!

The thought pulsed throughout my entire being. The weight of that terrifying realization sunk into me.

Chapter Five

SEPARATION

The weight of grief was suffocating, smothering me with every passing day. It was as though I was adrift in a sea of sorrow, with no lifeline to pull me back to shore. I spent hours sitting in silence, trying to find meaning in the senseless void left by my mother's passing. I lost track of time, lost track of myself.

Some days, I could barely summon the strength to get out of bed, let alone take care of my young daughters. It was as though the simple act of existing was too much to bear. On other days, I felt a fiery anger simmering just beneath the surface, a rage at the injustice of it all. But most of the time, I was just empty. A shell of a person, hollowed out by grief.

I knew I had to make a change. I had been working as a Home Care Case Manager, but after caring for my mother and watching her slip away, I knew I couldn't continue. The day she died, I hung up my nursing hat for good. My purpose as a nurse had been fulfilled, and I knew I had nothing more to give. My well was dry, and I had nothing left to draw from it.

Losing my mom just a month after my thirtieth birthday was a devastating blow. It was a double-edged sword, the pain of losing a child followed by the crushing weight of caring for a dying parent. It was a journey that left me drained and hollow, struggling to find my footing in a world that had been forever altered by loss.

In the aftermath of Gabriel's sudden departure, I was consumed with longing. The pain of not being able to say goodbye or express my love one last time haunted me for years. It was a shock that took its toll on me, layer by layer, as I struggled to come to terms with the trauma. I begged God to give me the chance to bid farewell to any loved ones should I face the same loss again.

But my mother's transition was a different kind of agony. It was a slow, agonizing decline that I knew was coming, yet I never knew when it would happen. Each loss of her independence, each day that her body deteriorated, was another blow to my heart. I had always imagined a magical moment when she would tell me how much she loved me and impart some final wisdom, but the reality was far from it. I never knew which conversation would be our last, and we all hung in the balance, waiting for that elusive moment.

I watched my mother suffer in ways no one should have to endure. I saw her fall again and again, only to pick herself up until she could no longer. But through it all, she taught me the incredible resilience of the human spirit, even when our bodies fail us.

Losing a child and losing a parent are two profoundly different experiences. Losing Gabriel shattered my hopes and dreams for the future, and the pain of missing him will never go away. But losing my mother felt like losing one of my best friends. She had been there for me from the beginning, cradling me in her arms, keeping me safe, and nurturing me. She was a confidante, an advisor, and a teacher. Now that she was gone, who would I turn to for advice?

During the months following Mom's death, I spent time with a therapist, hoping to unwind and unburden myself. The duration of Mom's illness had not been kind to my marriage; now, my soul was suffering. No matter how hard I tried to ensure both of my families were cared for, my conscience told me I'd failed to do enough.

Now, I had grown resentful.

I'd been caregiving for my parents, my young family, and my nursing patients, yet I had not received nor allowed myself to embrace that care in return. So often, I felt pressured to care for everybody else, thinking my spirit was invincible, and that I could do it all alone. I never asked for help. I became a martyr. Trapped in my own emotional whirlwind after Mom's death, unable to envision a peaceful, happy family life, I withdrew from my marriage.

Grief had taken its toll on every aspect of my life. My husband and I grieved in entirely different ways after Gabriel died and ended up on different paths. I had grown complacent in our relationship and believed that living like roommates was enough. We weren't taught how to grieve together, and fear kept us from communicating our deepest feelings. Barely adults, we didn't know how to navigate the deep waters of grief. We had experienced and endured a parent's biggest tragedy and didn't know how to hold each other through that.

With the crippling grief we had endured as parents, I still held an enormous amount of love for my husband, rivalled by a tremendous amount of guilt. Eventually, I abandoned my husband in his grief and pain because I could no longer ignore my own.

This led to the breakdown of our relationship. Instead of allowing myself to trust and lean into him for comfort, I grew the armor of a protective shell. Deep inside, I felt unworthy of love—though love was the one thing I wanted, it was the same thing I repelled.

Eventually, I abandoned my husband in his grief and pain because I could no longer ignore my own.

Despite having many discussions with my therapist about discovering my "new normal," I had yet to reveal my desire for a separation to my husband out of my own fear. I felt trapped in a role that no longer aligned with my true self, and this was taking a toll on me. As time passed, it became increasingly difficult to maintain the façade I had created, and I began to resent the person

I saw in the mirror. My inner voice was screaming for the attention and care that I had given to others but not received in return.

While my therapist and I had spoken for many hours about finding my own "new normal," I had not shared any of this with my husband. I was terrified to say the words, "I want a separation." I continued playing a role my heart was no longer willing to play—a role that came at my own ruin. Continuing the facade I'd created became harder and harder; soon, I resented the woman I saw staring back at me from the mirror. Inside I was screaming for everything I'd given to others and not received.

I was exhausted from living a lie.

Chapter Six

DIS-MEMBERING
TO RE-MEMBER

T he grizzly bear stood facing me, swiping its claw, head tilted back and roaring. I gasped out loud. I felt fearful yet exhilarated and completely alive, every cell in my body tingling.

My heart raced. With a deep breath, I came back to my body and opened my eyes. I was awake, and I was safe.

Seated on the floor in the middle of a workshop space, I drew inward to contemplate the meaning of the grizzly. The workshop facilitator led us on a guided meditation to help us connect to our spirit animal. I pondered the symbolism of the bear.

The Shaman gasped and took hold of my hands, her grip firm and unyielding. The words she spoke to me were like a laser beam, cutting through the air with razor-sharp precision. "I don't know what you've been through," she said, "but the grizzly bear is a fierce guide to have. Think about its paw - with one swipe, its claws shred everything in its path. Your path has been just as fierce. The grizzly spirit tells you that you must dis-member to re-member."

Her words shook me to my core, and for a moment, I struggled to catch my breath. I realized that the path of dismembering to remember would be an arduous one, full of trials and tribulations. But deep down, I knew that I had already begun the process of healing, and that it would require all the courage and strength I could muster.

My entire life was about to be shredded - physically, emotionally, mentally, and spiritually - but I was determined to rise from the ashes, like the fierce grizzly bear that had chosen to guide me.

Time and time again, I had to rely on the strength of the grizzly bear as my guide as I worked to dismember all the parts of myself and the trauma I had experienced.

As I boarded an airplane to fly home from this workshop in Chicago, a firestorm raged inside my mind: *It's over,* I decided, my heart skipping a beat. *My marriage is over.* The thought shocked me. My whole life, I'd dreamed of the perfect marriage—a home filled with children, a loving husband, and true happiness. I'd prayed for a relationship with my spouse that could overcome obstacles and prevail during difficult times—one built on honesty and trust. But the path to that dream marriage had proven to be more difficult than I'd ever imagined—

And it had become lonely.

I yearned for a better life.

Why are you doing this to yourself? My heart demanded. *Face it, Christy. It's over, and it's time for you to move on.*

Suddenly, an enormous weight lifted off my shoulders. *This is it,* I decided, closing my eyes as I melted into my seat on the plane. This decision had plagued me for years, yet I had always feared executing it. As the plane lifted off, returning home, there was no longer any question in my mind. Though triggering this decision would deeply hurt my husband, on a deeper level, my pleading mind was giving us both a gift.

I was setting us both free.

For two years, I had attended counselling, breaking down our relationship and attempting to rebuild it. My husband and I had endured eleven turbulent years of a marriage intertwined with grief and happiness. I realized something needed to change.

It would start with me.

When I finally gathered the courage to express my desire to separate, my husband was shell-shocked, blindsided, betrayed, and the last to know.

As I sat in my living room with my husband and daughters, my heart felt like it was being ripped apart. It was only a month before the first anniversary of my Mom's death, and I had just shattered my children's foundation of a family. I could see the confusion and sadness in their eyes, and I knew that I was the cause of it all. My husband sat next to me, tears streaming down his face, and I couldn't even bring myself to comfort him. I was too busy trying to keep myself together.

But in that moment, something shifted within me. I realized that I had been living in silence for far too long. I needed to speak my truth, no matter how much it hurt. And so, with a heavy heart, I spoke the words that would change our lives forever.

As I uttered those words, I felt a weight lift off of my shoulders. It was like a part of me had been freed, and I was finally able to see a path to healing. I knew that I had to face my brokenness, to retrieve all those shattered pieces of myself and mend them until they became scars. It was going to be a long and painful journey, but I was ready for it.

Just like the Japanese art of kintsugi, I would take my broken pieces and transform them into something beautiful. I would find the missing pieces and put them back together with gold, creating a masterpiece that was uniquely mine.

And so, I began my journey towards healing and wholeness, one step at a time.

Chapter Seven

MASKS

The decision to abandon my marriage led to unravelling the depths of the trauma I had experienced my entire life, from birth onward. Now on the heels of losing my son, my mom and my marriage, most importantly, I faced the difficult realization that in the process of every loss I had sustained, I had actually lost myself.

Struggling to find my new normal, desperate to find balance, in need of solitude and refuge instead of self-pity and pain, I returned to my steadfast protector, my best defense: hiding behind a mask.

I'd worn a mask to hide my true self all my life. I disguised my unhappiness behind a smile. I concealed my rejection behind a shrug. I cloaked my insecurity by creating distance. I hid my broken heart by pretending that everything was good and that I was strong.

As a child, I wore a mask to hide my emotion. Early on, I'd learned to hold in my emotions, stuff my feelings down deep and cage my anger behind a mask of self-control. Instead of venting my feelings, I silently buried them, deeper and deeper, letting them brew as long as possible until, eventually, my feelings exploded—a pattern I'd mastered throughout my life.

Silence was another mask.

In the battlefield of my adolescence, I was a prisoner of war, caught between two warring armies of masculine willpower. My father and adopted brother were each fighting for dominance and control, and I was the casualty caught in the crossfire. As my brother spiraled into a self-destructive path of drugs and alcohol, the tension and discord in our family grew unbearable. I felt powerless and suffocated, unable to speak up or stand my ground against the formidable forces around me. My desire for peace and neutrality only made me more vulnerable and lost in the chaos. The weight of my silence became a burden that crushed my spirit and drained me of my identity.

As a child, I felt like I was always trying to please others and live up to their expectations. It was as if I was wearing a mask, constantly putting on a show to make those around me happy. I felt like my own emotions didn't matter and were just a burden. I was a chameleon, changing my personality to fit in with different groups and avoid any conflict.

But inside, I was scared. I was scared of rejection and being alone, so I kept my true feelings to myself. I never spoke up for myself or stood up for what I believed in, always choosing to keep the peace instead. It was a constant struggle between my own desires and what others expected of me. And eventually, I felt trapped in my own body, like a prisoner unable to break free from the expectations of those around me.

Fake fearlessness was another mask.

The mask of a fearless overcomer—a strong, cheerful person who couldn't be beaten down by life—became a sanctuary for my grief, a protector of the pain I couldn't bear to feel.

Time after time, my masks protected me publicly from exposing my vulnerability and brokenness.

But behind the mask, I was a woman falling apart. Soon I ran out of ways to hide, and the masks began to crumble.

This was a blessing and a curse. Because where once I could hold my composure, I now entered new uncharted territory: vulnerability. I could no longer hide from myself or others. I needed help, and I needed it fast.

Counselling was my refuge, and I spent countless hours with a caring therapist. We made sense of my experiences, but the burden of my trauma prevented me from touching the deeper layers of my pain. The pain was unspeakable, and I needed something beyond counselling or prayer to help me through it.

I was broken at the age of 30.

I rejected my feminine nature, loathed myself, and felt unworthy of love. Separation was all I knew, from others, myself, and God. I was dismembered, trying to run away from my emotions, but deep inside, I yearned for connection and wholeness.

At first, I was overwhelmed by the number of loose pieces in my life. Asking for help was not easy, but I knew it was necessary. Everywhere I looked, there was raw emotion and unprocessed trauma.

But slowly, piece by broken piece, I began to heal. I realized how far I had strayed from my spirit. I had survived, but I was not thriving. I prayed to be whole again, and I was determined to make it happen. No longer able to hide from myself or others, I realized it was time to ask for help. I was exhausted, and I couldn't do it on my own.

Chapter Eight

ONE HEART

I am grateful to my parents for instilling in me the importance of pursuing holistic health care throughout my life. Along with visiting medical practitioners, I also sought the guidance of naturopaths and incorporated homeopathic remedies, vitamins and minerals into my health regimen.

Following Gabriel's death, I attended a wellness conference in Las Vegas. It was there, following a speaker's workshop, that I connected to Archangel Michael and Archangel Raphael profoundly. Their wisdom spoke to me on a deep level, and I felt a connection to the divine that I had never experienced before.

It was in the quiet of the night, alone in my bed, that I was able to confront the weight of my grief. I realized the density of my emotions, the power they held over me, and the impact they had on my physical body. But in that moment of clarity, I also discovered the power of healing. I shed emotional weight, and I knew that I had begun a journey of spiritual and emotional growth.

This experience taught me the importance of acknowledging and embracing our emotions, no matter how heavy they may be. It is only through this process that we can confront the truth of our experiences, find healing, and grow into the best versions of ourselves. The teachings of Archangel Michael and Archangel Raphael continue to guide me on this journey, helping me to find meaning in the midst of grief and pain.

Two years had passed since my mother's death, and I was still struggling with the weight of my grief. But when a friend suggested another workshop, this one on energy healing, I knew it was an opportunity I couldn't pass up. Without hesitation, I accepted and began making plans to attend.

I didn't know much about the teacher or the workshop, but I had a feeling that this was where I needed to be. Little did I know just how profound this experience would be.

When July finally arrived, I found myself at Miraval, attending my first energy healing and coaching workshop. As I watched the teacher work, I was both intimidated and transfixed. Her blonde spiked hair and petite hands seemed incongruous with the immense power she demonstrated in healing and transformation.

But as I delved deeper into the workshop, I began to understand just how transformative this experience would be. The teachings allowed me to confront the pain and trauma I had been carrying for so long, and to start the process of healing and moving forward.

This workshop was a turning point in my life, and I will never forget the impact it had on me. It taught me that healing is possible, no matter how heavy our burdens may be, and that we are all capable of transformation and growth.

I vividly recall the first healing transformation I witnessed that weekend. A man approached the stage and shared that he had been diagnosed with a cancerous tumor on his spine. As I watched Deborah work with him as a conduit of Spirit, I heard and felt a loud *snap* in his back. Seconds later, Deborah announced his process was complete.

I was awestruck. As each participant stood bravely revealing their own stories and reasons for being there, I noticed the common theme in each story. Each person sought freedom from their loss and release from past trauma while committing themselves to embark on a healing journey.

I was less courageous. It took me days to work up the courage to shakily raise my hand and ask for help—yet when the time arrived, I knew it was my moment of truth.

Grasping the microphone in my trembling hand, my voice quivered as I spoke my name. Terror of revealing myself surged through me. Only by the grace of God did I place one foot in front of the other as I moved to the front of the room and placed my hands in Deborah's.

There is a saying that "when the student is ready, the teacher will appear." This was that moment.

Looking into the audience, my voice shook as I let the unspeakably painful words out in the open: "My son fell through the ice and drowned."

Hearing a collective gasp from the crowd, I wanted to disappear into a black hole of grief. Then I felt Deborah's arm gently wrap around my shoulder. Suddenly a heavy blanket of pain lifted off me. Light began pouring in. As I recounted my story of death and loss, I realized I could face the world from this open-hearted space, freed from the burden of remaining silent. Watching the other attendees wipe away tears, I no longer felt alone. Each of us carried our own wounds, and each arrived for healing.

At that moment, I sensed we were all experiencing an awakening as if meditating together on the same rhythmic beat, a heartbeat that pulsated through the entire room. In that breathtaking moment, our hearts beat as one.

This healing moment is one that is etched in my heart. In this snapshot in time, I felt understood. Held. I knew that this day would positively impact my path to radical healing.

Chapter Nine

STOLEN INNOCENCE

After attending that workshop, I became aware of the impact that chronic and prolonged stress had taken on my body. I had been carrying an immense burden on my emotional and spiritual well-being for almost ten years, which eventually manifested as physical discomfort and dis-ease.

The toll of chronic stress on our physical, emotional, and spiritual well-being is a reality that many of us experience. It's not just an emotional burden, but a physiological one as well. The body's stress response is a natural survival mechanism that helps us deal with challenging situations, but when stress becomes chronic, the mind and body suffer.

The release of stress hormones, such as cortisol and adrenaline, during a stress response, is a vital physiological process that prepares the body for action. It increases heart rate, blood pressure, and respiration while redirecting blood flow to the muscles and brain. However, chronic stress can lead to an imbalance in hormone levels, which can have negative health consequences such as weakened immune function, digestive problems, and mental health issues.

As humans, we are complex beings with a dynamic energy field that surrounds us. This field is a network of interconnected energy layers that correspond to different aspects of our being, including our physical, emotional, mental, and spiritual dimensions. Our energy field is affected by the functioning of our organs, nervous system, and electromagnetic energy, as well as by our thoughts, emotions, and actions.

Energy healing is an holistic approach to wellness that focuses on enhancing the flow of energy through the body's chakras to promote physical, emotional, and spiritual well-being. By addressing disturbances in energy flow, energy healing can alleviate pain, illness, and emotional problems.

It's essential to take care of our emotions and experiences promptly, as unresolved emotions can become trapped in our energy bodies, creating blockages that disrupt the natural flow of our energy and emotions. By attending to our emotional health, we can promote the free flow of energy throughout our energy field, promoting optimal physical, emotional, and spiritual well-being.

After my mom passed away, my body began to show physical symptoms from the stress I'd endured. I had uncomfortable digestive issues and new food intolerances, and I had become accustomed to chronic back and pelvic pain and troubling ovarian cysts. The prolonged emotional stress had affected me in countless ways. But it wasn't just physical pain that I was dealing with.

I came to a stark realization that my physical body was also reflecting the emotional trauma that I had buried deep down inside of me. As a child, I had experienced traumatic events that were so painful that my brain had suppressed the memory. But as I coped with the deaths of my son and my mother, that buried trauma had resurfaced in the form of physical symptoms that I could no longer ignore. It became clear to me that I had to confront the many experiences, both remembered and suppressed, that were bubbling up inside me. It was a daunting task, but I knew that it was necessary for my own healing and wellbeing.

Keeping my emotions bottled up inside me was suffocating me. It was like holding my breath for too long. Eventually, those emotions had to emerge, gasping for air.

As a woman, my struggle to find peace has been a lifelong journey. Since childhood, I had buried my femininity beneath layers of shame, constantly grappling with feelings of self-condemnation and inadequacy. It was a war that waged both inside and outside of me, affecting my work and my relationships.

The memories of the sexual abuse I endured as a child still haunted me, and it was this trauma that led to my deep sense of revulsion towards my own femininity. To protect myself from further harm, I turned to food, using it as a way to numb myself from the pain. The weight I gained became a physical representation of the emotional burden I carried, and it seemed like the only way to shield myself from further abuse.

Of course, now, I can see that this was not a true form of protection at all. Rather, it was a way of dishonoring my own body, of denying the very essence of who I was. It was a painful and difficult journey, but I know that by confronting my past traumas and redefining my relationship with my body, I could finally find the peace that had eluded me for so long.

I stood at the grave weeping. I was 34 years old, visiting a tiny village in the Netherlands, 4,500 miles from home. This was the village my mother had grown up in. Standing over the granite gravestone, blinking away tears in the hot August sunlight, my insides felt tight and twisted.

When I embarked on this journey back to Holland, I had no idea I would end up in this place. The strength of violent emotion sweeping over every cell in my body took me by surprise. *Why did I come here?* I asked myself. The question clouded my eyes with tears, triggered my anxiety, and brought my mind back to an incident in the summer of 1985.

I was grieving. But not for the loss of the man buried in this grave. I was grieving for myself, for everything he had stolen from me.

My safety and security.

My health.

My self-image.

My innocence.

In the last 10 minutes, I emptied myself of hatred and resentment, all directed at him. Rage consumed me as I spat on his grave and called him vile, disgusting names. I cursed, repulsed at the memory of him. In this moment of brokenness, surrounded by the remains of my maternal ancestors, everything I had suppressed for so many years came rushing to the surface.

With each word I cried out, my heart grew lighter. The heavy burden and yoke I had been carrying dissipated.

When the rage simmered, and I ran out of words, I heard a quiet, gentle whisper in my soul. *Now you know what you need to do!*

My eyes closed, I breathed in and out slowly. *Oh God, I don't know if I can do what you ask me!*

The answer reverberated through my heart. *To forgive others is to liberate yourself and heal the past.*

Suddenly my body was covered in goosebumps, rolling in waves of lightness drawing upward. I drew in a deep breath, wiping away my tears. Today would be the day true healing began.

Today I'd take an important step. Today I'd find release.

Today I'd find *freedom.*

One summer when I was little, I was bubbling with excitement for our trip to Holland. It was my first big childhood adventure, and I couldn't wait to see my Oma and Opa for their 50th wedding anniversary. My Mom packed our suitcases with care, leaving space for precious souvenirs. She told me how much she missed her family, and I could feel her eagerness in the air.

The long flight felt never-ending, but my messy platinum blond ponytails and green eyes filled with wonder when we landed at Schiphol Airport. Meeting my grandparents, uncles, and aunts filled our hearts with joy. There were happy tears, and everyone remarked on how much my older brother and

I had grown. While my parents caught up with their loved ones, my brother and I found our own fun. Being in Holland was an adventure, from collecting snails to indulging in Dutch treats and visiting the famous children's amusement park. I felt on top of the world.

As we prepared for the big party, I admired myself in the mirror, twirling in my cute pastel dress, lacy socks, and brand-new shoes. I couldn't wait to dance, play, and laugh!

But little did I know, that day would change everything. It shattered the fragile emotional armor I had built and stripped away all of my future innocence.

As the party began and the crowd gathered at my uncle's farm, my family laughing and celebrating, I wandered around the farm, exploring. That's when I saw my uncle, who exclaimed how pretty I looked and took my hand, leading me into his shop.

It was there, at his farm, that my uncle used my trust in him as bait—to lure me in.

And to violate me.

As my uncle's hands roamed where they should never go, I felt frozen and powerless. My body was screaming for help, but my mind couldn't comprehend what was happening. I couldn't run or fight back; I was trapped in a nightmare that wouldn't end. The tears streaming down my face were a desperate plea for someone to save me, to take me away from this place. But when it was over, my uncle's silent gesture made it clear that I had to keep this a secret, that no one could know what had happened. I was alone with this burden, carrying it like a heavy weight that threatened to crush me.

As I stumbled towards my parents, my body convulsed with sobs, and I buried my face in their arms, seeking safety and comfort. But the words refused to come out, and I could only hold onto them as tightly as I could, hoping that their love and warmth would somehow erase what had happened.

In that moment, my entire world was turned upside down. Everything that I had once considered safe and secure was now tainted with fear and uncertainty. I felt exposed and violated, like a part of me had been taken away. The happy, carefree days of my childhood were gone, replaced by a haunting memory that I couldn't forget.

My relationship with my family was forever changed. I clung to my parents like a lifeline, terrified of being alone again. Every time they left my sight, my heart raced with anxiety and fear. I needed constant reassurance that they would return, that I wouldn't be abandoned.

My parents knew that something was wrong, but they didn't understand the depth of my pain. They teased me about my constant questions, not realizing that each one was a desperate plea for safety and security.

From that moment on, my world was consumed by fear. The fear of the unknown, the fear of the unexpected, the fear of being attacked again. Everywhere I turned, I felt like I was being watched. Every shadow, every sound, made my heart race and my palms sweat. My mind became a battlefield, and the enemy was the constant fear of what might happen.

Even the safety of my own bedroom could not ease my mind. I was convinced that someone or something was waiting for me under my bed or behind the curtains, ready to harm me. Each night, I prayed to make it through the night unscathed. My once peaceful and innocent world had been shattered, and I could never be sure of my safety again.

The darkness that had taken hold of me that summer remained hidden for years. The shame and guilt that I felt kept me silent, trapped in a cycle of fear and mistrust. But eventually, the truth would be revealed, and I could finally begin to heal.

As a teenager, my trauma deepened. I dreaded the monthly arrival of my period. It brought with it agonizing pain that I couldn't escape. I felt like my own body was betraying me, punishing me for something I didn't understand. The cramps were unbearable, and I would often end up curled up in a ball, crying in pain. The only relief came from lying in a hot bathtub, but even then, the pain lingered, a constant reminder of my femininity.

As I grew older, the pain became more than just a monthly inconvenience. It was a physical manifestation of the abuse I had suffered at the hands of my uncle. The trauma had seeped into my body, settling into my reproductive organs, causing years of pelvic issues and chronic pain. It was like a dark cloud that hung over me, a constant reminder of what had happened and what I couldn't change.

The shame was overwhelming. I felt like I was somehow responsible for what had happened, that I had somehow brought it upon myself. It was a heavy burden that I carried alone, afraid to speak out, afraid of being judged or rejected. It wasn't until much later that I realized that the shame wasn't mine to bear. I had done nothing wrong, and the abuse was not my fault.

My body had become a battleground, the physical manifestation of the emotional turmoil I had endured for years. The surgeries were just a Band-Aid, a temporary fix for a deeper issue. It wasn't until I faced the emotional pain head-on, acknowledging the trauma and processing it, that I began to heal. The physical pain began to ease as I released the emotional weight I had carried for so long.

Inhale. Exhale. Inhale. Exhale…

Many years later, as an adult, I was at home, in my bedroom, recovering from surgery to remove my right ovary. I sat cross-legged on my bed, the pain medication wearing off, trying to focus on my breaths to fight off the throbbing pain.

Inhale. Exhale.

Stubbornly the pain refused to quiet. Negative thoughts clouded my mind as I continued counting my breaths, consciously attempting to bring breath to the pain.

Why isn't this working? What is my body trying to tell me?

Over the years, my body defied every conscious attempt I made at healing. Time after time, the surgeon's knife had carved away the physical aspects of the emotional and mental anguish I stored in my womb. Yet even the skilled hands of the surgeon couldn't heal me.

Physically, emotionally and spiritually, I needed to undertake that inner journey to finish carving away what the surgeon couldn't. And I needed to make the first cut myself.

Seated on my bed, trying to breathe away the pain, I hardly knew where to begin. Over the course of 10 years, I had faced down one surgical procedure after another: three caesarean sections, a uterine ablation and tubal ligation, a hysterectomy, the partial removal of my left ovary, and now the removal of my right. It was like knocking over dominoes—first one surgery, then another, watching each one fall in succession. Increasingly, I learned to separate and dissociate from my feminine organs. I quelled any thoughts that I was punishing myself, rejecting my feminine nature. The thorny truth was that I loathed myself to the core of my being.

The truth was screaming at me as I recovered from the latest ovarian surgery. Now as I tried to control my fear by breathing: *Inhale. Exhale.* I heard that truth loud and clear.

The pain and suffering I endured now have a visible reminder, too: A physical scar that sliced my body from hip to hip.

That scar was with me all these years after the original wound was inflicted as I stood over my uncle's grave marker in Holland. I thought back to the five-year-old girl in brand new shoes and two blond ponytails—the girl who had felt powerless and abused. Finally, after many years, I could release that little girl from her cold, dark prison cell. I could tell that little girl that she might have been abused, violated and robbed, but she was not broken. Nor were her wounds beyond repair. These scars were on the mend.

That little girl could be set free now by sharing the grace and mercy of a prayer:

Forgive them, Father, for they know not what they do.

Chapter Ten

THE DIVINE FEMININE

W ith every step I took, I could feel my inner wounds screaming out for healing. The pain that had been etched deep inside me was too much to bear. I knew that in order to heal, I needed to take a journey deep into the Amazon, to the heart of the jungle, and immerse myself in the healing power of nature.

As I walked with the shaman, I could feel myself becoming more and more connected to the wisdom of the natural world. The trees, the plants, the animals—they all seemed to hold a secret knowledge that I was desperate to uncover. And as we worked with the plant medicines, I felt my body slowly beginning to heal.

One night, as I lay under the stars, I could feel the weight of all my pain and sadness crushing down on me. Tears flowed freely from my eyes as I sobbed uncontrollably. I cried for every woman who had ever been hurt, for every woman who had ever felt like she wasn't enough.

But in the midst of my pain, I felt a sense of connection to something greater than myself. I felt the Divine presence of the Mother, holding me in her loving embrace and reminding me that I was not alone.

That night was a turning point for me. I realized that in order to truly heal, I needed to embrace my femininity. I needed to let go of the shame and pain that I had been carrying for so long and accept the beauty and strength that came with being a woman. My womb was not a place to store pain and fear—it was a sacred space that was meant for love and new beginnings. And so I embraced my femininity, with all its softness, sensuality, and strength. I allowed myself to be vulnerable, to be compassionate, to be nurturing. And in doing so, I found a sense of peace that I had never known before.

My opportunity to slice away yet another layer of shame from my sexual abuse came at another energy healing workshop in Los Angeles.

Banded together with other women, each of us wounded by catastrophic events we'd been powerless to control, I felt surrounded by the healing energy of the Divine Mother. Each of our circumstances and experiences was unique. However, there was a deep resonance in each of us. As their voices spoke love over me, urging me to let go of the past and express my true self, a hard knot of unforgiveness inside me unravelled. And the healing words I desperately needed tumbled out:

I don't know how to fix this part of my life. But I can face it and start today by forgiving myself.

Suddenly I realized that beneath my shame lay decades of anger: molten, hot, scalding lava. I screamed in anguish as I tore through each painful, burning layer of unexpressed emotion. Compounding the perpetrator's energy locked inside me was layer after layer of self-punishment. I punished myself for my shortcomings, blamed myself for what happened to me, and manifested years of chronic pain. Forgiving myself wasn't an option I'd ever entertained.

Now, on this day, one of the most important of my life, it was the option that might save my life.

After the workshop, I took time to journal, speak to my body, and offer gratitude once I found none. I allowed myself to grieve for the losses of my femininity, both physical and emotional. I shifted my perception from the pain I had endured as a result of the dysfunction of the organs to compassion and love that despite it all I carried the gifts of three beautiful children. I honored the wisdom and gifts my womb and ovaries brought me. I extended my prayers and gratitude back to Mother Earth. I surrendered the grief, shame and pain I had suffered and placed it at the feet of the Divine Mother, knowing it no longer served me.

As I stood before the mirror in my bedroom, I couldn't believe my eyes. The reflection staring back at me was no longer the same wounded, shattered woman I had known for so long. Instead, I saw someone who was calm and content, at peace with herself and her experiences. For the first time, I could appreciate the beauty of the scars, both physical and emotional, that I had carried for so long. I knew then that I was not unworthy of forgiveness or love.

In that moment, I realized that it was time. Time to silence the vicious self-talk that had plagued me for so long, time to embrace my inner strength as a woman, and time to end the internal battle I had been waging against my own body.

From the depths of my soul, I yearned to understand the Divine Feminine. This sacred energy represents the feminine aspect of divinity, embodying traits such as nurturing, intuition, empathy, creativity, and wisdom. It is the perfect balance to the traditionally masculine portrayal of the divine, which emphasizes strength, power, and control.

As I delved deeper into my studies, I realized that current societal imbalances are a direct result of an overemphasis on masculine traits and a neglect of feminine ones. The only way to restore balance is to renew our focus on the Divine Feminine.

The healing properties of the Divine Feminine are powerful and transformative. They can help us tap into our nurturing, compassionate, and intuitive qualities, often associated with feminine energy. Through connecting with the Divine Feminine, we can experience a sense of inner peace, harmony, and wholeness. This is particularly helpful for those of us who have experienced trauma, emotional pain, or a disconnection from our feelings and intuition.

The Divine Feminine is often associated with the archetype of the mother. She provides comfort, support, and unconditional love. By connecting with this archetype, we can heal our inner child wounds and cultivate a greater sense of self-love and acceptance.

Moreover, the Divine Mother is deeply connected to the cycles of nature. She provides guidance and wisdom for those seeking healing. By connecting with the rhythms of nature, we can learn to live in harmony with the natural world and cultivate a profound sense of balance and grounding.

As I continued my journey, I studied many Divine Feminine healer archetypes. I found within myself the same energies present in the stories and legends written throughout history. I discovered the powerful healer and lover in Mary Magdalene, the nurturer in Mother Mary, and the mighty warrior in Isis. With a vested interest in this sacred energy, I continue to deepen my connection with the Divine Feminine.

I invoked the power of the great Egyptian Goddess Isis. Her presence surrounded me, and I could feel her nurturing and protective energy embracing me. As I focused on her image, I drew upon her strength and resilience, hoping to embody her qualities and overcome my own obstacles.

Isis was known for her magical abilities, and I could feel her powerful presence throughout many aspects of my life. I felt as though I too could call upon her for protection, healing, and assistance. As a guardian of sacred knowledge, she was revered for her wisdom and ability to teach humanity essential skills. I felt as though I too could learn from her, tapping into her knowledge to find answers to my deepest questions.

But it was her love for her beloved that resonated with me most deeply. She collected all the severed, scattered pieces of her lover Osiris and resurrected him with her love. The sheer force of her love brought him back to life. If she could love him back to life, I wondered, could I not symbolically do the same for myself?

In that moment, I felt a deep sense of gratitude for Isis's love and compassion. As I opened my heart to her, I knew that I too could love myself back to life. With her strength and resilience as my guide, I felt empowered to overcome any obstacle that lay in my path. Isis's enduring legacy continued to inspire me, and I knew that she would always be there to guide and protect me.

When I first turned to Mother Mary, I was feeling lost and alone. Her image, often depicted holding her Son, brought tears to my eyes. I could feel her motherly love and care radiating from the image, and I knew that she was someone who could offer me the comfort and support that I so desperately needed.

As I delved deeper into her story, I was struck by her forgiveness and her willingness to offer solace to those who were suffering. I admired her humility and her devotion to her faith, and I felt inspired by her strength and resilience in the face of adversity. I knew that if anyone could understand my own pain and suffering, it would be her. She, too, lost her son.

In that moment, Mother Mary became like a mother to me. She offered me the consolation, understanding, and compassion that I had been seeking. I knew that I could turn to her in times of need and that she would always be there to offer me guidance and protection.

Through my connection with Mother Mary, I found a renewed sense of hope and purpose. Her strength and resilience inspired me to be more compassionate and forgiving, and her motherly love and care gave me the courage to face the challenges of life with grace and dignity.

As I opened myself to the energy of Mary Magdalene, the "other" Mary, I felt a profound sense of understanding and connection. Her teachings and healing abilities have been revered for centuries, and it was easy to see why. She embodies the qualities of unconditional love and compassion, which can be powerful tools in the process of healing. Through her teachings, she encourages individuals to embrace their pain and transform it into opportunities for growth and awakening, offering empowerment and inner strength to those who seek her guidance.

Mary Magdalene's teachings also remind us of the power of the divine feminine within ourselves and others. Her wisdom encourages us to honor and embrace our feminine qualities, helping us to connect with the Divine and access higher states of consciousness. As a spiritual teacher and guide, she offers a pathway to healing and transformation.

For me, Mary Magdalene's teachings and healing qualities were especially powerful, as I discovered my voice and my own ability to heal. I felt a deep resonance with her story, knowing that she too had been silenced and suppressed by the patriarchal system for many years. Her journey inspired me to reclaim my own power and embrace my feminine qualities.

In addition, Mary Magdalene had also experienced a profound loss, grieving for someone she loved deeply. This knowledge deepened my connection with her and helped me to find solace in her teachings. Through her example, I was able to find strength and resilience in the face of my own challenges and heartbreak.

As I faced my own pain and wounds, these Divine Feminine figures became my source of inspiration and hope in the healing process. I imagined Mother Mary and Mary Magdalene in the tomb after the crucifixion, their hearts heavy with grief as they tended to their Beloved's body. I could feel their love and tenderness as they gently cleansed His wounds and anointed His body with precious oils. It was a delicate and sacred act, one filled with love and devotion.

In that moment, I realized that I could trust these loving women to tend to my own wounds and help me heal. I surrendered to their nurturing presence and allowed them to wrap me in their love, placing healing balm where it was needed most. It was a powerful and transformative experience, one that brought me closer to the Divine and reminded me of the power of love and compassion.

Weeks after my last pelvic surgery, standing in front of my bedroom mirror, my reflection staring back at me, I delicately traced my fingers along the line of scarring from hip to hip across my abdomen. Suddenly I was hit by a wave of tears. In the mirror, I witnessed a woman who had survived many intense battles on every level of my field—physical, mental and emotional. Each trauma had left a mark, a wound, a scar.

In the mirror, I saw a grown woman who had survived many intense battles—a woman who'd clawed and fought her way out of every corner life had backed her into. Each trauma she'd faced and overcome left a mark, a scar.

I traced the old scars on my body, the years of cuts I'd healed. As I stared at myself, I realized that my *scars are beautiful.* Every scar spoke of the struggles I withstood. My abdominal scars were no longer only a physical reminder of the pain and trauma—they were scars of victory, proudly bearing witness to the warrior inside. My scars told a tale of liberation and forgiveness. Each cut on my body was a brush stroke of paint on my canvas, enhancing the masterpiece.

No longer defined by my past or controlled by my anger, I chose to walk in grace and into the open arms of the Divine Feminine, my true essence.

No longer would I be at war with my body, and I could confess my love for it. These scars and wounds are who I am.

Beautiful. Fierce. Strong. Loving.

I'm not the pain, and I'm not the shame. I can let that go.

Hands shaking, I traced my battle scars, the pieces of my past. Eyes closed, I took a deep breath.

I emptied my mind.

I silenced the lies.

I awakened the roar of the Divine Feminine within.

Chapter Eleven

BORN WITH A
BROKEN HEART

The Divine Feminine had opened up a pathway for me to explore and understand the feminine and maternal aspects of my being, and I felt drawn to this journey despite my trepidation.

The loss of my mother was a devastating blow, leaving me feeling like I had been cast adrift in a sea of pain and grief. I was overwhelmed with the sense that I was now an orphan, with no one to turn to for guidance or comfort. But the truth was, this wasn't the first time I had experienced the pain of abandonment. From the moment of my birth, I had been separated from my biological mother, and now, once again, I had been left behind by the person who had taken me in and raised me as her own.

It was a wound that had never fully healed, a shadow that had followed me throughout my life, and I knew that it was time to face it head-on. I needed to confront my fear of being alone and unloved, to delve deep into the emotional pain that had been simmering beneath the surface for so long. It was a daunting task, but I knew that it was necessary if I ever hoped to find true healing and wholeness.

These thoughts weighed heavily on my heart, and I couldn't take this decision lightly. But I knew that I had to be brave and face my fears, no matter the cost. I had developed the tools and strength needed to cope with whatever I found, and it was time to take that next step towards healing.

A thick, heavy envelope sits cradled in my hands. It holds a secret that has haunted me for as long as I can remember.

Looking at the postmark— GOVERNMENT POST-ADOPTION REGISTRY—I attempt to relax. But the trembling in my fingertips grows. This envelope holds the key to my identity and lineage, my life's deepest mystery, the final piece to completing the puzzle of *Who am I? Where do I come from?* That both frightened and excited me.

For decades, I had been plagued by a gnawing curiosity about my origins, my biological family. I yearned to know my roots, to hear the story of my conception and where I came from. Today, holding this envelope in my fingers, I feel a step closer to understanding.

A million questions and a thousand possibilities flooded my mind. *Am I better to leave the past in the past? Do I really want to know what this envelope contains? What if the answers bring even more questions? Do I really need this on top of everything else I am dealing with? Or should I persevere, no matter the cost? There is no going back. If I open it, I can't "unsee" it.*

Deep at the core of my being, I felt unlovable, unwanted, unfit, and undeserving.

Through all the loss I'd experienced, I believed that even God had deserted me.

Despite the contentment and love I received from my adoptive family, I wrestled with these chaotic thoughts year after year. I became a daughter, a woman, a wife, and a mother—and yet the facts about where I came from eluded me.

Now I cradle this envelope and stroke the tears from my face. As I do, I feel the earth shift under my feet. I find the courage to face the moment of truth at my fingertips.

Time to bring the necessary healing, I tell myself. *Time to face whatever is inside.*

As I tear open the seal, out spill the documents. I take a deep breath and prepare to read the names of my birth parents. Fresh tears spill as my eyes land on my birth parents' names—names I'd yearned to know, names which pieced together the story of my unknown family. How I've longed to know my roots, lineage, and ancestry.

It's a strange sensation to absorb the names of the two people who came together to conceive me. I repeat their names until I have them committed to memory.

I'd invented and imagined so many different stories for years but seeing it in black and white is surreal. In the blink of an eye, my birth parents become real, and my fictional stories dissolve. Like a sponge, I absorb every letter in these documents. I read until my eyes sting until the words are a blur.

Now I can compare my own physical and personality traits to theirs, smiling to see what's trickled down the genetic line.

My heart was racing as I typed my birth mother's name into Google, eager to uncover the truth about my past. As I scrolled through the search results, my eyes locked on an adoption registry. And there it was - a post from my biological father, looking for me. My mind was spinning as I realized that I had stumbled upon the man who had played a role in my conception. This was not the way I had envisioned finding my birth parents, and my nerves were on edge as I considered what this meeting would mean.

I reached out to my biological father, my fingers shaking as I hit the send button.

Months later, I sat in my truck outside the restaurant where we had arranged to meet. My stomach was in knots as I considered the fact that I was about to come face-to-face with the man who had walked away from me so many years ago. *Would we have anything in common?* These were questions that had plagued me for years, and now I was about to get the answers.

As I stepped out of the truck, my heart was pounding in my chest. I took a deep breath and walked towards the restaurant. The waitress brings me to the table on the sunny patio outside. Seated, there is the man whose face I've been searching for forever. When I saw him sitting there, it was like looking into a mirror. He smiled at me and we awkwardly hugged, both of us unsure of what to do next.

As we sat down to talk, my nerves began to settle. He was down-to-earth and easy to talk to, and we quickly found common ground. Learning that I had three half-sisters only added to the sense of wonder and curiosity that I felt. But there was still one question that remained unanswered - where was my birth mother?

Even though our time together was brief, it was liberating to finally connect with the man who had been looking for me for so many years. As we hugged goodbye, I felt a sense of peace and contentment wash over me. And yet, I knew that there was still more to discover about my past - and I was ready to face whatever came next.

Finding my birth mother proved to be more difficult. Eight years after receiving my adoption papers, I still came up empty each time I searched her name. I resisted the thought of hiring a professional to search for her.

In hindsight, it was I who resisted moving forward. I held back, not knowing what I truly wanted from our interaction. I envisioned something tense, hushed—a radically different experience than meeting my father. Sometimes I'd wait a year or two between Google searches as if locking what little facts or clues I had in a time capsule. Still, she was often in my thoughts.

As I continued my healing and the years passed, I realized I unconsciously harbored resentment toward her—and, in turn, toward myself. To a certain extent, I blamed my biological mother for the circumstances in my life and her unwillingness to protect me. It took years to realize this was irrational, but it was a shadow that needed to find the light so I could set both of us free.

On another level, I feared she might reject me again. I yearned to know my roots, yet I hesitated and retreated time and time again. I had trouble summoning the courage to take the leap of faith in finding her.

I knew life would never be the same once I found her. Surely, she wouldn't be happy to meet the biological child who appeared out of nowhere to disrupt her life. No matter which road I chose, it felt like a risk.

Finally, one day, I found a lead to her when my biological grandfather's obituary filled my Google search. Although my birth mother's last name was not listed, I knew this was her family, as my birth father had shared her parents' names with me. Still, I waited for two years before discovering the courage to reach out to my birth mother's mother. Realizing she was 88 years old, I knew that time might be running short and that I may lose the only lead I had found on the trail to discovering my biological mother. Knowing this was the one rock I had not yet turned over in my healing, although I was scared, I knew I had gone as far as I could in my journey and this was a necessity. I had to face my fear of rejection. It took conscious effort to let go of any expectations.

My heart racing, I came home from work for lunch one day and compulsively decided to reach for the phone to call my biological grandmother. I was terrified I'd give her a heart attack. *What if she knew nothing about me?* With a giant leap of faith, I pressed the green call button on my iPhone. I introduced myself, awkwardly explaining who I was and timidly asked if she was aware I existed. A guarded voice responded, "I think so… but I thought you were a boy!" As we eased into the conversation, my biological grandmother quickly warmed up and began sharing many details about my birth mother who like me, had been pregnant at age 19. I learned I had two more half-sisters. My birth mother played banjo along with her dad, and my biological grandmother played piano. I soaked in all of this new information.

I could now attribute my musical roots to my maternal side of the family. Something that had trickled down the genetic line to me. I could sense my biological grandmother's pride hearing how music connected us all. Perhaps this was where my inherent love for music originated. It felt exhilarating to know that I too had similar characteristics to those I shared DNA with.

Nearing the end of the phone call, I shared my contact information with her, and she told me she would contact my biological mother to see if she would want to have any contact with me.

Immediately I felt I had lost control of the situation. *What if she never contacted me?* I needed to take a deep breath and surrender this to Spirit. It was beyond my control. I needed to find peace quickly, as I might never have a response.

Months later, the buzz of my iPhone stunned me. Clutching the phone in my hand, I watch as an incoming text message popped up on the screen. I blinked; a grainy old photograph appeared, sent by my birth mother. Transfixed, I bent as close as possible to the screen and stared into my own eyes.

It was me. My own baby photo.

I gazed in shock, in disbelief. Tracing my finger over the color image— over my infant's face, my baby hair, my newborn cheeks—the room around me seemed to shudder, and a sudden wave of dizziness hit me.

Take a deep breath, Christy, I tell myself. *Relax.*

I had never entertained the idea of this photo existing. Now it appeared to me transcending time and space in a fraction of a second on my cellphone. I feel stunned.

In the photo, my birth mother and I are together in a sterile white room in a hospital. She is dressed in a housecoat, half-smiling and holding me. I'm wearing a little white newborn hospital gown. My tiny baby legs are crossed, my arms open wide, ready to embrace, receive, be cuddled, be loved, and be accepted. Here in this snapshot, the two of us are together, and the incandescent child in her arms dreams of a shared future, unaware her life is about to change.

The photo from my birth mother takes me back nearly 40 years, and it rewinds time to my first hours of life, my beginnings. Letting my thoughts drift away momentarily, I cup my palm over the phone, and sit on my couch, knees trembling.

In the next hour, I will speak to my biological mother for the first time. I pause, letting my emotion completely overwhelm me, tears streaming down my face. When I awoke this morning, my life was as I had always known it. Now, a 40-year-old photograph I've never seen stares back at me—infant eyes crinkling into a smile, cheeks flushed bright pink.

It is bewildering to look at this face. Yet seeing this little girl, I feel relief, joy, and something inexplicably beautiful. I sense a bond, a connection, and I sense this little girl is drenched in grace.

Did I know in this moment I'd never be held again by my mother? My heart breaks in wondering.

Mysteries, doubts, the unknowing—they have always been my story. In this photo, we are connected. Yet the seams that held our lives together are about to unravel. Moments after the photo was snapped, my mother would leave, and I would be swept away into the arms of nurses, doctors, social workers and strangers.

This is the dance I have known all my life: The dance of abandonment, the dance of disconnection, and the dance of striving to hold onto something, anything.

As a newborn, I wasn't aware I was being left behind, that my mother and I would be ripped apart the next moment.

At birth, I'd emerged from the security of my mother's womb with the umbilical cord wrapped around my neck, choking me. My eyes opened for the first time to the hospital's bright, loud, chaotic environment—to being poked and prodded, shaken and scrubbed, swaddled and bundled. Instantly, life became a battlefield.

I was placed in the hospital nursery for the first three weeks of life. In those early days of my life, the echo of vibrating machines interrupted my slumber. The throbbing of doctors' and nurses' voices pulsated as they entered and exited the room.

My basic needs were met—yet my primordial connection was severed. Alone, wide-eyed, frightened by the intense sights and sounds of my surroundings, I longed for my mother's loving voice to soothe me, her arms to rock me, and the soft smell of her skin to connect me to that loving touch.

I am thankful for the nurses who lifted me out of my bassinet to rock me in comfort and feed me.

But sometimes…

Sometimes I wonder if my life would have been different had I experienced the warm and comforting arms of a mother and father to shelter and nourish my every need in those first hours, days, and weeks of life instead of nurses. Instead of medical technicians. Instead of social workers.

Instead of *strangers.*

Separation wasn't my only issue.

I was born with a broken heart—specifically, a heart murmur, a septal defect. Over time, this defect would become deeply symbolic. It became my deepest wound.

My adoptive parents were aware of this defect. When I was 20 days old, a social worker placed me in the arms of strangers. The man was a hard-working Dutchman with fiery red hair and wild eyebrows who held a deep and steadfast faith in the power of God. He was 31, a hard-working dreamer born in Holland, who immigrated to Canada with dreams of farming and wide open space. He had a loud voice and a strong will, achieving anything he put his mind to. The woman was 29, taller than the man at nearly six feet. Shy about her height, and also originally from Holland, she was more of a quiet but strong, behind-the-scenes type. Her voice was quiet and her touch gentle. Together, they farmed wheat and sunflowers. They poured their blood, sweat and tears into the land as they built a life they felt worthy of living.

Trembling with anticipation, they drove 3 hours, from the small rural town they lived in to the city to meet me for the first time. Unable to conceive biological children of their own, they had excitedly chosen to adopt. With my 18-month older adopted brother, we would become a complete family of four. Finally, I would be safe in the arms of a father and mother, a family who would accept me as their own, who would embrace me, protect me, and love me.

The social worker advised my new parents to undress me that day, inspect me, and decide whether or not to keep me. "After all," she warned, "the girl was born with a handicap"—a defective heart. Stricken, my parents did as instructed. They later say they saw nothing except perfection.

I was a transaction to the social worker, like choosing fruit at the supermarket. Take it or leave it, bruises and all. Inspect the goods and decide if it's good enough.

I later realized this moment propelled me to become a people pleaser. As time went by, it became deeply symbolic. This trauma of needing to be perfect to be worthy of love and acceptance became part of my identity. It became a deep wound. So deep, I was unconscious of its intensity. I believed if I behaved perfectly, looked perfect, and spoke perfectly, I would gain favor. I would be loved. Accepted. I would be safe. Not abandoned. Yet the more I attempted to please others, to be the perfect version of what I felt they wanted, to gain their love and acceptance, the deeper I abandoned who I authentically was to become what others needed me to be. I abandoned myself.

But for now, at this moment as a tiny infant, I could finally savor the feeling of loving arms, a protective home. Through unconditional love, the man and woman who came to meet me instantly became parents. I finally had a mother and father who would always be there, who could wrap me in safety. Content, I knew I was finally safe. My new home became my safe cocoon.

I was surrendered into the arms of love.

Their love nurtured me as a toddler, offering healing balm to an abandoned heart. But even their love couldn't prevent bad things from happening.

As a young girl, I suffered from recurrent strep throat. While in our local hospital, being prepped for a simple tonsillectomy, the doctors discovered my heart valve was leaking. In shock, they told my parents they could not proceed with the tonsillectomy as initially planned.

Instead, I would need urgent open-heart surgery.

Heart surgery! Instantly my parents were bombarded by confusion. *How could this be?* They wondered. My heart murmur was medically cleared when I was a month old and followed yearly by my physician as a precaution. For no reason they could understand, my vulnerable heart had sustained valve damage, likely due to recurrent strep infections.

In a flurry, I was admitted to the same hospital where I had been born, the same sterile building where I had been taken from my birth mother's arms.

The day before surgery, to comfort this frightened child, the nurse read me my favorite book, *Bunny Follows His Nose.* At the same time, my doctor sliced an incision in my leg, carefully threading a camera through my femoral artery into my heart. "It's okay, honey. It'll be over in a moment," the nurse whispered, gently stroking my brow. Yet all I wanted was my parents. *Where are they?* I heard myself groaning.

For the next 24 hours, I wasn't permitted to bend my leg; it was secured with gauze to a stiff board to keep it straight. Pain and fear ripped through me. I shifted my weight, trying to move and find a comfortable position. Finally, I broke down in tears. I felt trapped. I wanted to be like the other six-year-olds, playing with my friends at school and watching TV at home with my family. Instead, I was confined to a cramped hospital bed, listening to the echo of the ticking clock as I agonizingly awaited the moment I would be wheeled into surgery.

The rest is a blur. I woke from sedation groggily, in the bright, noisy recovery room and I ached all over. Bolts of agony shot through my chest. All I wanted was my parents. *Where are they?* My mind screamed. Although there were nurses everywhere, I felt scared and alone. The surgeon had warned my parents it would be a time-intensive procedure, advising them to leave the hospital to catch their breath.

I spent the next two weeks in the hospital. Because I was a young girl with soft bones, the surgeons opted to go in through my posterior rib cage and repair my heart. Recovery was painful, each movement reminding me of the first physical scar I carried. My only solace came in the form of a purple popsicle—my spirit leapt every day when the therapist swept into my room with this sugary treat. Savoring the grape flavor produced a happy and comforting childhood memory—and now a distraction from the discomfort of excruciating recovery.

This was my first visible scar—my pierced heart.

Decades later, sitting alone on my living room couch as I recovered from my latest pelvic surgery, cradling the cellphone that holds the newborn picture of myself, I replay these memories. As I do, I start to feel a shift. This photo was sent by a stranger—my birth mother. A 40-year-old photograph from the woman who carried me in her womb. A woman I have never known.

Seeing this photograph allowed me to finally believe in the story I had always wanted to. I was surrendered out of love. I was content. Peaceful. At that moment, resentment is released. Forgiveness is granted. There is a moment of integration where I begin to free myself from the haunting shadows of all those painful events and dense emotions. Tears of relief streamed down my cheeks. Weight lifts from my shoulders. The tightness around my heart eases as warmth spreads through my veins. A deep breath frees my lungs from the cage they have been in. Peace begins to settle in.

My eyes caught sight of the six-inch scar from my childhood open heart surgery. I thought back to the girl I was then, at age six, and the broken heart I'd been born with. I realized that during those weeks of recovery in the hospital, there were angels—compassionate messengers of love—stepping in to protect me. All of the times I thought I had been abandoned and alone, now I saw the guiding hand of Spirit surrounding me through every dark moment in my life.

The woman in this picture is now offering me a precious gift. She has unburied this treasure to share with me, and she is revealing to me her own hidden truth. Through this token, she offers reconciliation and an answer to my prayers. I see an opportunity to build a bridge to heal.

This is the woman who brought me into being, I think, as I curl up in my seat, my body shaking as I gaze into her, face. *I waited all these years to find you. Will my broken heart finally be healed?*

For 40 years, we both built up walls and pushed each other away. Now, we are both on a path never taken. We are putting a wrecking ball to the past. We are shielding our eyes from the shards of brokenness that once swirled around us, and we are offering our hearts up, in childlike innocence, no longer as a gauntlet, but as a gift.

My heart pounded so hard in my chest, I could hardly think straight. After years of wondering, dreaming, and searching, I was finally pulling into the parking lot of the hotel in the town where my birth mother lived. The anticipation was overwhelming, and I felt like I was about to burst with emotion.

But as I stepped out of the car and looked around, everything seemed so unfamiliar and intimidating. The world was suddenly a foreign, magical, and sparkling place, but at the same time, it was a place that scared me to my core. *Was I really ready for this? Had I made a terrible mistake?*

My nerves were frayed, and my mind was racing with questions. *Should I hug her? What if she didn't like me?* I found myself obsessing over every detail of my appearance, as if that could somehow make up for all the years we had been apart. But then, something clicked.

As I looked at my reflection in the mirror, I felt a newfound sense of strength and courage. I didn't need to prove anything to anyone. I didn't need to be perfect. All that mattered was that I was here, in this moment, ready to meet the woman who had given me life. And even if it didn't go perfectly, even if there were tears and awkward silences, I knew deep down that I was enough.

I took a deep breath and walked out of my hotel room, feeling a sense of purpose and determination. The search for acceptance and acknowledgement was over. I had found it within myself. And with that, I stepped into the unknown, ready to face whatever lay ahead.

It was a life-changing moment. The realization dawned on me that all that really mattered was that I accepted and loved myself. Though I had always known this, it was the first time I felt it with all my heart. It was devastating to realize how much I had neglected myself and looked for validation from others. It's crucial to be seen, heard, felt and loved, but ultimately, I was searching for my own self-love. I had never needed anyone else's approval to feel complete.

As I drove to my biological mother's house, I felt a newfound sense of confidence.

I parked and approached the front door of her home. The house appeared quaint and well-cared for. She was a gardener, something else we had in common. In the front garden, I noticed the skulls of large animals. *A hunter's home,* I surmised. Now I was more curious than ever, and I wondered what secrets lay behind her door.

When I rang the bell, there was no response, and I started to worry. *Had she changed her mind about meeting me?* Then I heard footsteps, and the door opened. I saw my birth mother for the first time, and our eyes locked.

My shoulders tensed as I waited for her to say something. I asked if I could hug her, and we both embraced. It was such a relief to finally be there. A fluffy cat purred by my feet, and I noticed all the photographs and cross-stitched pictures on the walls, made by her mother. The space felt cozy and inviting. As she guided me through her home, I felt a surge of gratitude and compassion for the woman who had struggled so much in her life.

For nearly six hours, we talked and shared everything that had made us who we were. We laughed and cried, sharing our biggest fears and realizing how much we had in common. It was an extraordinary day. She invited me back for brunch the next day.

I felt proud of my upbringing and grateful for the values of perseverance and integrity that she had instilled in me.

For the first time in my life, I felt secure in who I was. I no longer questioned my worth. Self-worth is all about recognizing our value and uniqueness, setting healthy boundaries, and pursuing goals with confidence and determination. Low self-worth had held me back for years, but all the meditation, prayer, healing energy, and inner work had prepared me to meet my birth mother from a place of love and not as a wounded, abandoned child.

As we hugged goodbye, I felt content and at peace. There was no awkwardness or tension.

Stepping outside, a feeling of awe washed over me at what had just transpired. As I returned to my truck, softly, gently, I heard my birth mother's voice cut into my quiet contemplation: "Please text when you get home safe."

In that moment of expanded awareness, the broken pieces of myself came together as a whole. I had never been rejected.

With a smile, I assured her, "I will."

Back home again, relaxing in the warm Jacuzzi tub after an emotional day, I reached over to pick up my phone. Holding it steady in my hand, I scrolled to the digital photograph of my birth mother and me, snapped 40 years ago, in the moments before our separation. Staring into my newborn eyes, tracing my finger over my infant cheeks, my heart expanded in awe and wonder. Every difficult question I yearned to ask felt divinely answered.

No longer do I feel rejected. No longer do I feel abandoned.

In this moment, staring into my image, my beginnings, everything I had ever known to be true falls into place. Broken puzzle pieces of my past are collected and restored. I understand my journey. I have been graced by the miraculous, and I have found myself. Finally, I can know it, live it, and *feel* it.

I am held.

I am worthy.

I am loved.

PART TWO

"You are the abyss that opens beneath you and the bridge you have to cross. You are the cave you need to find and occupy, the heart that holds the eternal fire. And resting there, you will realize that you are the cloud floating in the heavens, the rain falling, and then evaporating once again. Then you will know God."

- Lars Muhl

Chapter Twelve

SURRENDER

I n the journey of healing, we often find ourselves navigating through
twists and turns. It's a non-linear path that takes us through the deepest
and darkest places within ourselves. But along the way, something magical
happens. Our consciousness expands, and we discover light where we once
saw only darkness. It's a beautiful journey of transformation that unfolds in
a succession of moments.

As we move forward, we begin to witness ourselves. We observe our
experiences, emotions, and thoughts without judgment or avoidance. The
powerful practice of bearing witness involves being present with ourselves
and taking responsibility for our feelings and actions. It's not an easy task, but
with self-reflection, mindfulness, meditation, and journaling, we can become
more aware of our thoughts and feelings and develop greater self-compassion
and self-awareness. It allows us to recognize and accept our own vulnera-
bilities and limitations, which in turn, can help us develop greater empathy
and compassion for others.

Along my journey, I discovered the power of vulnerability. Allowing
myself to be vulnerable and open was a powerful tool for healing emotional
wounds and cultivating emotional resilience. It required me to be honest
and authentic with myself and others about my emotions, experiences, and
needs, even when it felt uncomfortable or scary.

Being seen as I truly am without the need to hide behind masks or defenses was a liberating and empowering experience. It allowed me to connect more deeply with myself and others. Vulnerability helped me confront and process difficult emotions and experiences, such as trauma, grief, or shame. By opening myself up to these emotions and experiences, I was able to release them and move through them rather than suppressing or avoiding them.

Vulnerability can be challenging, but it can also be transformative. By embracing vulnerability, we can cultivate greater emotional resilience, deepen our connections with others, and ultimately live more fulfilling and authentic lives. It's a journey worth taking, and the rewards are immeasurable.

Surrounded by the tranquil healing at Miraval in Tuscon, Arizona, I booked an appointment with an Ayurvedic practitioner at the spa one evening after another expansive energy healing workshop. As warm oil poured over my forehead, I relaxed, at peace, my mind drifting off. All at once, I felt God's presence envelop me in a warm embrace. Tears trickled down my cheeks.

"I thought you had forgotten about me," I pondered sadly to my Creator.

I waited, listening. In a voice as familiar as my own, I heard: *My dear child, how could you possibly think I had forgotten you?*

In an instant, the weight of my past slid off my body. Overwhelmed by this unconditional love, I surrendered to it, seeing each broken piece of my life falling into place. Only a power greater than myself could heal this.

As a young girl, I held faith in abundance—in many ways, faith was *all* I had to hold onto. I found comfort with the Angels, Saints and Archangels in my darkest moments. With Mother Mary, I found peace, and in Jesus, I found strength. As a child, the ritual of Sunday Mass was always warm and comforting, and I found a home and protection in the Church.

As a wounded adult, I pulled away from the Church, as my childhood faith disappointed me. I felt abandoned and judged by other Church members, and I no longer found the Church to be my refuge, my home.

One Easter not long ago, I reluctantly agreed to go to Good Friday Mass with my dad. As the Mass began, I felt like I was sitting inside a pressure cooker. Unwilling to listen to the sermon, I distracted myself, letting my eyes wander to the beautiful stained glass surrounding me. Suddenly, bursting through my thoughts, one word from the priest caught my attention:

Surrender.

As his voice faded away, I meditated on that word. *Surrender.* Surrendering had been a difficult process for me—even though I accepted that life becomes easier without resistance. Focusing on that simple word, *surrender,* I felt a shift inside. Tears started streaming down my face. Instantly my anger with God subsided, and His love poured in its place.

At that moment, the comforting voices of the harmonizing choir behind me began singing, "Be still, and know that I AM."

That's when it hit me: I was a free woman—free to reject the lies I told myself about my broken life. This was Divine timing to surrender the burdens I had been carrying.

I've been trying to do this alone, I thought, *instead of surrendering into the arms of the One who knew me the best, who would always guide and protect me.*

My trauma had served as a wall, a barrier preventing me from experiencing a deep and intimate relationship with myself, others, and the Divine.

It was a revelation to discover I'd never been alone. Loss is inevitable. Darkness comes to us all. Yet even in the dark, we are never alone—in fact, we are even more surrounded. The deepest dark brings the greatest Light.

Chapter Thirteen

BORN ANEW

Higher spiritual values are the principles or qualities significant in pursuing spiritual growth and enlightenment. These values are linked with developing a deeper connection to one's inner self, a greater sense of purpose and meaning in life, and a heightened awareness of the interconnectedness of all things. Higher spiritual values include (but are not limited to) love and compassion, forgiveness, gratitude, humility, integrity, service, and inner peace. These values are fostered through spiritual practices such as meditation, prayer, and contemplation and can lead to a more profound sense of fulfillment, purpose, and meaning in life.

I would love to tell you that forgiveness is as simple as snapping your fingers. Unfortunately, as you know, it is more complicated. Sometimes forgiveness bears many layers and conscious intention. In my case, not only did I need to forgive others and God, but also myself. That was a massive realization as I recognized the necessity of forgiving myself. I never realized how difficult I was on myself. I constantly chastised myself for not knowing better, for not being better, or stronger, or thinner or prettier. I could not love myself fully until I could learn to forgive myself for treating myself in a detrimental manner. And if I couldn't love myself, I couldn't love another. Once I brought my conscious awareness to that, I could no longer ignore the elephant in the room.

There are so many available tools for practicing self-love. And the most important thing is simply making that commitment to yourself. Take that first step towards self-love, whatever that may look like to you. With self-love comes an improvement in feelings of self-worth, allowing us to create healthy boundaries, particularly with relationships. Where once we may have been a doormat, now, the self-confidence is present to know you are worth so much more.

When we experience trauma, we tend to forget those higher parts of ourselves that existed prior to the experience. By coming into contact with the emotions resulting from the trauma, we release all those things we are not. We are not our trauma.

One of the most difficult challenges we encounter in life is to not cower during a storm, but to stand tall, courageously knowing our heart might break from the winds of change but that a shattered heart can mend.

When we accept this challenge, keeping our hearts open with conscious intent, the shattered pieces of ourselves begin to mold back together, forming a new and beautiful masterpiece. A new normal. We focus on what we have and who we can embrace instead of who or what is missing. A new world opens if we shift our focus from despair and grief to gratitude and humility. Our hearts become a strong fortress. Hearts open wide, and we face every challenge head-on. We transform the pain and suffering into unconditional love.

Every single moment of our lives is an opportunity to be born anew. Each moment offers us a choice to experience peace, seek and discover who we really are. Every one of us are imperfect creations. If we can look at ourselves from the template of perfection, not judging our emotions or thoughts, we'd no longer feel so weighed down by the experiences and trauma we encounter.

By operating from a place of gratitude, we can raise our vibration. This takes a mindful approach to finding space to be grateful no matter our situation. If you are someone who struggles to find gratitude in the ordinary,

I challenge you to grab a paper and pen and start a daily practice of writing down just three things you are grateful for. It can be as simple as being thankful for a cup of coffee, a smile from a friend, a warm coat or a beautiful candle. As you retrain your brain and bring awareness to everything that surrounds you, you can find gratitude in the most minute details throughout your day. Eventually, that list of 3 grows to infinite on any given day, and the positivity multiplies and radiates.

The personal growth my losses have inspired has been overwhelming at times, however, I am deeply humbled to be able to reflect in gratitude for each experience of love I've encountered. I have been blessed, despite all else, to experience love, compassion and joy.

When gratitude meets grief– peace, love and compassion descend. We realize what an incredibly precious gift life is and are meant to live it fully and freely. Encouraged, we seize every precious moment in faith, happiness, and love.

I often think about Gabriel as he looked out the farm's living room window as the Christmas lights lit up the darkened sky.

Childlike wonder is the stuff of dreams and magic, a state of being that ignites the imagination and fills the heart with boundless joy and curiosity. It's the purest form of enchantment, a reminder that the world is full of wonder and mystery waiting to be discovered. It serves as a reminder that there is always something new to discover and learn and that the world is full of mystery and wonder *if* we are willing to seek it out.

Unlike adults, they are not yet weighed down by life's responsibilities, pressures, or life experiences. As we mature, we tend to lose this sense of wonder and curiosity as we become more preoccupied with practical matters and the challenges of daily life. However, it is possible to recapture this childlike wonder by cultivating an open-minded and inquisitive approach to the world, embracing novel experiences, and allowing ourselves to be surprised and delighted by the unexpected.

That childlike wonder is a state I intentionally connect to, especially in times of stress, finding gratitude and unencumbered presence in each moment. Remembering that innocence deep within and the joy that bubbles up is something that gave me the strength to keep putting one foot in front of the other.

I remember with joy walking into the kitchen one day and noticing a sliver of light. As I opened the door, Gabriel sat with his legs crossed, holding a spoon, sporting a huge dripping grin and half a watermelon plopped on his lap.

When I put on one of his favorite movies, Gabriel would clap his hands excitedly. As the music played, he'd open his arms wide, spin, dance, and laugh until he tumbled to the floor. He curled up on my lap during the sad parts, wanting comfort. He lived and embraced every emotion. What an incredible gift to live so fully embracing each moment life offers. Feeling the full spectrum of emotion and allowing it to be exactly what it needs to be.

This small snapshot in time captures the essence of the way I choose to live my life, unapologetically authentic and grateful with a smile radiating joy while surrendering to waves of sadness and tears as they arise.

This reminds me of a time when my daughter, Annika, was about 3 years old. She was terrified of putting her head under the water. At swim lessons one day, I sat on the bench near the side of the pool as she surrendered, finally willing to dip her head below the surface of the water. As she emerged, wiping the water from her eyes she turned toward me, the biggest, brightest smile on her face and waved. Transfixed at that moment, I glimpsed Gabriel in her essence, in her radiant joy at overcoming her biggest fear, and I heard him whisper, "Look at me, Mom! Everything is ok!" With pure, unapologetic joy, Annika fearlessly dunked her head again and never looked back, fully embracing the ecstasy of choosing love over fear.

Chapter Fourteen

SERVICE

The transformative power of service is undeniable. Through acts of service, we can turn our pain and trauma into something empowering and positive, unlocking a greater sense of healing and well-being.

Being of service means going beyond ourselves and offering a helping hand to those in need. It can involve anything from volunteering at a soup kitchen, to tending to a sick pet, to offering support to a friend in need. By being helpful and positively impacting the lives of others, we can experience a sense of purpose and meaning in our own lives.

Through service, we can develop new skills, build stronger relationships, and feel good about ourselves. But perhaps the most important benefit of being of service is the opportunity to connect with others and make a positive difference in their lives. By reducing feelings of isolation and loneliness, we can experience a powerful sense of belonging and fulfillment.

For those struggling with social isolation or depression, being of service can be particularly beneficial. By developing greater empathy and compassion for others, we become more understanding and supportive, leading to a powerful healing impact on our physical, emotional, and spiritual well-being.

Ultimately, being of service is a way to contribute to the well-being of the world around us and to make a positive difference in the lives of others.

Following the multiple losses in my life, I began seeking opportunities to be of service. It wasn't something someone told me I should do; it was just something my soul asked me to explore. I had an enormous void I needed to fill and no idea where to start. I began by volunteering in my daughter's classrooms when they were younger and taking a fundraising chairperson position on the school council. I joined the Board of Directors for a local sports association.

I continued to find true healing at an orphanage near and dear to my heart in Peru in 2011, a few short months following Mom's passing. My family had long been involved in paying it forward and helping others. For many years I organized and coordinated my dad's team to travel to various places in South America to build orphanages. In 2011, the year following Mom's passing, I desperately yearned to attend personally. It was the first of many profound healing journeys.

The catalyst was that I had been blessed to go on a mission trip, years before, with my mom and dad to Guatemala. Volunteering to fundraise, buy materials and construct orphanages was something my dad had done for several years before my mom and I had an opportunity to join him. On this trip, I realized I was pregnant with my youngest daughter. This trip to Guatemala was about three years after we lost Gabriel. While my mom had found solace in snuggling the babies and toddlers, I avoided the pain of seeing children around the same age Gabriel was when he passed. I devoted my time to the teenagers instead volunteering in the school or just going out and getting my hands dirty constructing new buildings and laying bricks. The physical labor kept my mind occupied and my hands busy, which at the time provided a positive distraction from the deep feelings of grief I was experiencing.

Skipping ahead a few years,, following Mom's death I was ready for a change in environment. I wanted to get away from it all. The sense of responsibility still plagued me I felt in her care. All those months after her loss, there were still days I would begin walking down the hallway to her room before realizing I no longer needed to check on her. So embedded was the routine of taking care I sometimes neglected to remember she was no longer resting in her room. During this time, I was also struggling with the indecision about ending my marriage. Grief had changed me. It had changed the way I was able to connect with others around me. It became increasingly difficult for me to find common ground with my husband. We were no longer grieving together. Our grief pulled us apart. So, this trip was great timing for me to get away and attempt to clear my head in the hopes of finding some clarity.

For several years, I had been coordinating these groups to visit the orphanage in Peru. However, this would be the year I would take the reins and begin group-leading myself with a charity near and dear to my heart. I was so excited to embark on this new adventure to Peru. Of course, adding to the appeal was the prospect of visiting one of the Wonders of the World, Machu Picchu. At the time, I never realized it would be the first of 7 trips to Machu Picchu and 14 trips to Peru thus far.

It is hard to explain, but when I landed on foreign soil in Lima, I somehow felt at home. I *knew* this place. There was a richness in the eyes of the locals. They did not have much, but they were rich in spirit; a wisdom they carried that felt ancient.

As I landed in Lima and boarded our bus to travel to our campsite at the orphanage, my excitement was a breath of fresh air. Arriving at the orphanage for the first time in a town 2 hours from Lima was one of the most heart-opening experiences I've had. The simplicity of outdoor showers and toilets, sleeping on the ground in a tent and communal meals under the shade from the sun brought unexpected healing.

I had thought that my expansive home, king-size bed, granite countertops, and luxurious cars provided me comfort. Yet, beneath the vast Peruvian night sky, I let go of all the baggage I hadn't even realized I was carrying.

For the first time in a very long time, I felt like me, before any of the trauma. I connected deeply to my essence and inner light, the *me,* before anything happened. It was blissful. With exuberance, I sat in the noisy lunch hall while the kids excitedly shared and we ate simple meals together. I did not expect this time at the home to be as magical and profoundly healing as it was, and I had found renewed purpose and joy.

From that day forward, Peru became a sanctuary, a hallowed and healing ground for me. Each trip back to Peru brought a deeper inner journey, another layer of healing which helped reconnect with the deep parts of myself I had long ignored or forgotten. In addition, I found a family and a sense of belonging, of being part of the greater whole.

I felt a deep pull to sponsor a sixteen-year-old boy who had made an enormous effort to connect with me. Something in my gut told me he would play an important role in my life. With tears streaming down our cheeks, we realized as we shared our stories that we were brought together by no accident. His brother had drowned, just as my son had. His father had died, just as my mom had. I knew deeply that this child had been brought to me to help me heal another layer of loss.

I will never forget the profoundly emotional moment when he said, "I hope that God gives to you what you have given to me." I had no idea what this boy's story was before that evening, and it was yet another synchronistic event in which I felt the universe had conspired, bringing him to me, so we could heal collectively. Grateful tears streamed down my face as I heard his words as I realized God had actually given me the gift in bringing this special young man into my life, to bring me healing.

He was one of many people along my healing path who held the lantern for me in my darkest moments. Despite our suffering, we recognize pieces of ourselves in others, and we can connect soul to soul, bringing healing.

Being present with over 100 children at the home in Peru, all suffering the same core wound of abandonment, allowed me to open my own in vulnerability and courage. Although our wounds were so similar, we had completely different circumstances. The locals experience a lack of support, education and a struggle for survival. Seeing them, I realized how fortunate

I truly was. A real connection unfolded when I encountered my new godson and learned about his trials and suffering. It made me realize that when we share similar wounds and meet others in their pain, at a point in time where we can be there for others who are experiencing the same things. I realized every single relationship became a reflection of where I was on my healing journey.

My heart brimmed with compassion for those I met along the way. And yet, everyone I encountered carried this depth in their eyes. I realized, visiting these people who had lived on the land for generations, that there was beauty, richness, and deep wisdom in the simplicity of their slow-paced lives.

I wondered what life would be like without all of the busyness, complications, and tasks we do to keep ourselves busy and appear important. I grieved that we as a society had lost the art of connection and were too busy to notice each other and connect heart to heart. I vowed to take this new awareness home with me.

The other thing I noticed on my subsequent visits to the home in Peru was that because of the inner healing journey I had committed to, the more I opened my heart to these children and staff, the more their hearts opened in return. When I return to the home now, I hear the chorus' of "Tia! (Auntie)" being called out whenever I'm spotted, while they run and jump into my arms for a hug, and it gives me a renewed sense of lighthearted joy.

There were a million extraordinary moments I experienced with the kids at the home. The experiences in Peru were rich in healing balm for my wounded soul and abandoned heart. Being of service gave me purpose, understanding, and faith in something much more significant than myself. I felt a sense of belonging. I found healing in many small moments, in giving of myself, in giving and receiving gratitude, and love, and experiencing joy in the core of my being.

One year, on the anniversary of my Mother's death, I stood outside the newly constructed baby house that my dad had generously funded and built in remembrance of my mom and her love of children. I could feel my mom's presence with me that day as we celebrated this new beautiful space for children, who like me, had been abandoned. Knowing Mom's legacy included providing a safe, warm and caring environment for these babies, lessened my own pain and opened my heart in ways unimaginable.

Chapter Fifteen

HEALING TOOLBOX

Our life experiences can take us to the deepest, darkest places within ourselves. Healing from trauma is a complex process that varies from person to person. Losing someone or something you deeply care about can be a painful and challenging experience. It is natural to feel a range of emotions, such as sadness, anger, confusion, and even numbness. However, it is essential to understand that healing from loss is a process that takes time. Unfortunately, there is no magical formula that can erase or eradicate the pain. But there are many different tools that can be utilized throughout the process of healing to assist in finding a peaceful state within yourself.

It's important to seek support from trusted friends, family members, or a therapist. Practicing self-care, such as getting enough sleep, eating a healthy diet, exercising, and engaging in enjoyable activities, is also important. Grounding techniques, like deep breathing and mindfulness, can help you stay present and connected to the moment.

Forgiveness can also be a powerful tool for building resilience and personal growth as well as releasing anger and resentment. Through forgiveness, individuals can transform their pain into a source of strength and wisdom and use their experiences to help others who may be going through similar struggles.

Finding meaning and purpose in life can also help you move forward after trauma. It's essential to be patient, compassionate and kind to yourself throughout the healing journey and to seek support as needed.

Taking care of yourself is a crucial aspect of healing from emotional pain or trauma. Grief and other emotional stressors can take a toll on both your physical and emotional health, making it essential to prioritize self-care activities. My story illustrates that grief can take a toll on various levels of our entire being.

One key aspect of self-care is maintaining healthy habits, such as eating a balanced diet, getting enough sleep, and engaging in regular exercise. These activities can help to improve physical health and boost overall well-being.

Spending time with loved ones is another important aspect of self-care. Social support can play a vital role in the healing process, providing a sense of connection and validation. Whether it's spending time with family, friends, or a support group, connecting with others who can offer empathy and understanding can be incredibly beneficial.

Self-care also involves setting healthy boundaries and learning to prioritize your own needs. This may involve saying no to activities or commitments that are not aligned with your values or priorities, or taking time to engage in activities that bring joy and relaxation.

Reaching out for support is an important step towards healing for those who have experienced trauma or emotional pain. It can be challenging to share your feelings and experiences with others, but doing so can be a helpful way to process emotions and receive support.

Family, friends, or a therapist can offer a listening ear and provide a safe and supportive space to express oneself. Talking through difficult emotions with a trusted individual can help to alleviate feelings of isolation and loneliness and can provide a sense of validation and understanding.

Therapy can be particularly helpful for individuals who have experienced trauma, as it can offer specialized techniques and strategies for coping with difficult emotions and processing trauma. A therapist can also help individuals to develop new skills and coping mechanisms and can provide a space for individuals to work through any underlying issues that may be contributing to their emotional pain. Sharing your feelings with others can be a helpful way to process your emotions and receive support.

One of the most challenging things to do is to find meaning in the loss, which can help in coming to terms with it. Reflecting on what you have learned from the experience or how it has helped you grow can be a meaningful exercise and may help you to find a peaceful way forward.

After a loss, it can be helpful to create a new routine. This can provide a sense of structure and stability in your life. Finding a new normal involves adapting to a different way of life that reflects the reality of the loss. This may involve adjusting daily routines, making new connections, or pursuing new interests and goals. It's a process of creating a new sense of meaning and purpose that can help individuals move forward while honoring the memory of the person they have lost. Grief can be a long and complicated journey, and there is no set timeline for finding a new normal. However, with time, patience, and self-compassion, you can find a way to live a fulfilling life while honoring the memory of your loved one.

Be kind to yourself and understand that healing from loss is a process. It is essential to give yourself time and space to grieve. Practice self-compassion. Ultimately, self-compassion is about treating yourself with the same level of kindness and care that you would offer to a friend or loved one, promoting greater healing and well-being.

Remember, healing from loss is a continuous process, and there is no "right" way to grieve. Everyone experiences loss differently, so it is important to be patient with yourself and seek support when needed.

Chapter Sixteen

ENERGY HEALING 101

Energy healing has the power to bring light into the darkest parts of our souls. It can be a beacon of hope for those who feel lost and over-whelmed by their negative experiences and emotions. The beauty of energy healing is that it doesn't require us to relive or confront our traumas head-on. Sometimes, we may not even be aware of the situations that are being healed.

When I think of energy healing, I am reminded of a scene from the movie "The Shack" where Sarayu, the Holy Spirit, takes the main character to the garden of his soul. The garden is overgrown and complicated, full of both flowers and weeds. Sarayu reminds the main character that it's a work in progress, and with love and patience, anything can be tended to.

For me, energy healing is a powerful tool that helps remove the weeds of negative experiences and emotions from our inner gardens. But it's import-ant to understand that our dense emotions serve a purpose in our lives. They propel us forward, helping us grow and learn. However, if we get stuck in those emotions and can't move through them, we may create issues for ourselves in the future.

It's crucial to give ourselves permission to feel our emotions and not judge ourselves for them. Emotions like sadness, anger, guilt, and even relief are all normal and valid. Instead of running from them, we should acknowledge and accept our feelings, sit with them, breathe into them, and let them move through us. This way, we can heal ourselves and tend to our inner gardens with love and compassion.

The human energy field is an intricate system of energy centers, known as chakras, that each hold unique power and characteristics. From the base of the spine to the crown of the head, these chakras govern our physical and emotional well-being, and their balance is crucial for a harmonious life.

The first chakra, the Root Chakra, is the foundation upon which we build our lives. Located at the base of the spine, it governs our sense of grounding, stability, and connection to the physical world. When this chakra is balanced, we feel safe and secure, with a strong sense of belonging to our families and communities. But when it's blocked, we can feel lost and disconnected, with a sense of anxiety and insecurity that affects our survival needs.

The second chakra, the Sacral Chakra, is like a fountain of creativity and pleasure. Located in the lower abdomen, it governs our emotions, sensuality, and sexuality. When this chakra is open and flowing, we experience joy and creativity, expressing ourselves freely and without inhibition. But when it's blocked, we may feel emotionally unstable, with a lack of creativity and even sexual dysfunction. We may also feel guilt or shame for expressing our desires.

The third chakra, the Solar Plexus Chakra, is like a blazing fire within us. Located in the upper abdomen, it governs our personal power, self-esteem, and willpower. When this chakra is shining brightly, we have the confidence and strength to pursue our goals, asserting ourselves with clarity and conviction. But when it's dimmed or blocked, we may feel powerless, lacking in self-confidence and direction, with physical symptoms such as digestive issues and fatigue.

The fourth chakra, the Heart Chakra, is like a loving embrace. It is the center of love, compassion, and empathy. Located in the center of the chest, it governs our ability to give and receive love, both for ourselves and others. When this chakra is open and balanced, we experience a deep sense of connection, loving and accepting ourselves and others unconditionally.

But when it's blocked, we may struggle with loneliness and isolation, finding it hard to express our emotions and form close relationships.

The fifth chakra, the Throat Chakra, is like a clear, powerful voice. Located in the throat, it governs our communication, self-expression, and creativity. When this chakra is open and flowing, we can communicate effectively, expressing ourselves with authenticity and clarity. But when it's blocked or unbalanced, we may struggle to speak our truth, with physical symptoms such as a sore throat or neck pain.

The sixth chakra, the Third Eye Chakra, is the center of intuition and perception. Located in the forehead, it governs our ability to see beyond the physical realm, connecting us to our inner wisdom and spiritual truth. When this chakra is open and balanced, we experience clarity and insight, with a deep sense of purpose and direction. But when it's blocked, we may struggle with confusion and indecision, feeling disconnected from our inner guidance and intuition.

The seventh chakra, the Crown Chakra, is the highest and most spiritual of all the seven chakras. Located at the crown of the head, it governs our connection to the divine, our sense of unity with all things. When this chakra is open and balanced, we experience a deep sense of peace and harmony, with a profound understanding of our place in the universe. But when it's blocked, we may feel disconnected from our spiritual nature, with a sense of disorientation and lack of purpose.

Our bodies are the vessels through which we experience life - every joy, every pain, every trauma, etched into our flesh and energy system. It can feel like a never-ending battle, with each experience leaving a scar on our physical and emotional being. But we don't have to be prisoners to our past. We have the power to heal ourselves and restore balance to our body, mind, and spirit.

By understanding the role of each chakra, we can identify where we need healing. We can face our fears, confront our traumas, and release the negative energy that holds us back. This allows our life force energy to flow freely, connecting us to the universal energy that unites all living beings - Source.

Connecting with Source feels like plugging into a cosmic power grid, where we feel a sense of purpose, belonging, and unity. We become aware that we are not alone in our struggles and that we are part of something greater than ourselves. We can unlock the infinite potential of the universe and realize our own potential for enlightenment, healing, and personal growth.

However, this isn't an easy journey. It takes courage, persistence, and determination. We need to confront our shadows, embrace our true selves, and let go of patterns and beliefs that no longer serve us. We must treat our body, mind, and spirit as a whole and not just address the symptoms.

When we understand the effects of our experiences: body, mind and spirit, we are better equipped to seek healing. As we can bring ourselves into balance, our life force energy flows easily, and things align and move with ease and grace. This also allows us to connect deeper into the vast field that is Source. This term refers to a divine or universal energy that is the origin of all life and creation. This energy is the ultimate source of all existence and can be called God, the Universe or Consciousness.

Source is the underlying force that connects all living beings, and as such, it is a unifying and empowering force. We can achieve greater enlightenment, healing, and personal growth by tapping into this vast energy field. By aligning ourselves with the universe's positive energy, we can bring about positive changes in our lives and the world. It is a powerful and transformative force that can help us connect with our higher selves, achieve greater levels of consciousness, and tap into the universe's infinite potential.

Within us lies a depth beyond our physicality, personality, and ego: our Higher Self. This facet of our consciousness is inextricably connected to the universal energy of the universe, allowing us to access boundless wisdom and comprehension. Our Higher Self serves as our spiritual guide, closest to the source of all existence.

To connect with this aspect of ourselves, we engage in techniques such as meditation, visualization, or prayer. These practices grant us access to heightened levels of intuition, creativity, and inner tranquility. As we delve deeper into our Higher Self, we begin to unravel our true nature and our place in the cosmos.

This journey of self-discovery can spark a spiritual awakening, a transformative shift in our consciousness and perception. It involves a heightened sense of awareness and a deepening of our spiritual beliefs and practices. This awakening can arise spontaneously or through significant life events, both positive and negative. Intentional spiritual practices like meditation, prayer, or yoga can also lead to an awakening.

As we undergo a spiritual awakening, we may experience a range of emotions, from euphoria to confusion to fear. We may also feel a stronger sense of connection to ourselves, others, and the universe, leading to a renewed sense of purpose and meaning in our lives. This awakening inevitably leads to various changes in our lives, including shifts in our relationships, career, or lifestyle choices. We become more compassionate and empathetic towards others, and our desire to serve the greater good amplifies.

I prayed for a way to bridge my medical, emotional, and spiritual training into a means of helping others. Little did I know that Spirit had a different path in store for me, one that would lead me back to nursing after the loss of my mother and the end of my marriage. Initially, I saw this as a practical necessity, but I soon discovered a new-found passion for end-of-life care. The experience of losing loved ones had a profound impact on me, and I felt called to use my skills and knowledge to make a difference in the lives of those facing the end of their own journeys.

As I made my way to the hospital for an appointment with one of my patients and their palliative care doctor, I decided to enter through a different door than my usual route. I had no idea that this detour would lead me to a moment where I could serve as the bridge I had prayed to be. Spirit had other plans for me.

A young man in his twenties stopped me, asking if I could point him to the "detox" unit. I accompanied him and little did I know that this encounter would take a sharp turn.

It was no accident that I crossed his path.

The next moment, he collapsed into my arms and it seemed he was near death.

Pinned between the wall and his body, heart to heart, I could feel his life force leaving, followed by what I can only describe as an electric shock that coursed through my own heart. I later learned this young man had overdosed, getting one "last hit" before going into detox.

Without hesitation, I sought help to lay him down and immediately began CPR. Thanks to the medical team, he was revived. I strongly believe that Spirit had a reason for bringing him back and that I was merely a bridge, doing what was asked of me. It was a perfect marriage of my medical and spiritual training, tending to his physical body while allowing Spirit to use me as a conduit for his spiritual healing. The experience was nothing short of incredible.

I made a commitment to Spirit to be of complete service whenever needed, and that day, Spirit put me to the test. The experience was a beautiful healing not only for the young man but also for me.

This experience awakened my own realization: that the time for change is *now*. If we wait for the future, we may not have another chance. How often do we say, "I'll do that tomorrow" or "Just one more time"? Tomorrow may never come.

The future is not promised.

We know that the time for a change, the time for healing, is *now*.

We need to slow down to take time for what is most important.

Throughout my career, I have engaged in deep and meaningful conversations with patients and their loved ones. One of the most significant topics we discuss is the balance between the quality and quantity of life. Together, we explore their values and beliefs to better understand their wishes and preferences. Some people prioritize extending their lives for as long as possible, even if it requires aggressive medical interventions, while others prioritize living a shorter but more purposeful life. Ultimately, it is a deeply personal and subjective choice, and my role is to support them in making the decision that feels most aligned with their own values and beliefs.

Working alongside my step-sister, Karla, as she battled cervical cancer was an experience that touched me to my core. Her strength and resilience in the face of such a devastating illness was nothing short of inspiring. As I watched her navigate her journey with grace and dignity, I couldn't help but feel humbled by the lessons she was teaching me.

Through her personal writing and our intimate conversations, I was given a glimpse into the world of illness and end-of-life care. Witnessing her transition from a mindset of cure to one of acceptance and surrender was both heartbreaking and beautiful. And even as she faced her own mortality, she remained steadfast in her determination to make a difference in the lives of others.

After her passing, I found myself seeking solace in a healing workshop surrounded by the tranquil beauty of the redwood forest. It was there that I experienced a profound moment of healing and connection with Karla, as I felt her vibrant and joyous energy surrounding me. In that moment, I knew that she was healed and whole, and it brought me a sense of peace amidst my grief. This is how our loved ones who have passed want us to experience our lives while we are here, on this earth, completely present in our bodies, rooted in our earthly experience. Dancing with joy. With light. With love. Her legacy lives on as a testament to the incredible strength of the human spirit.

I came to understand that healing doesn't always manifest in the way we anticipate, and that it is not always synonymous with a cure. These concepts can be challenging to grasp, as we are conditioned to believe that medicine is the solution to our health problems. In the medical field, we are not always equipped with the tools to cope when treatments fail. It requires a certain level of skill to release our attachment to being cured and embrace the idea that we are already healed, even if it takes a different form than we imagined.

One day, I stopped in my young palliative patient's hospital room, aware that his time was drawing short and that it was time to say goodbye. I asked him if he had any regrets or something he wished he could have done. He was courageously strong, under age 30, and said, "I have lived a good life and am ready to meet whatever comes next." Awestruck at that moment, I wondered, if I were in his place, *would I be able to answer with the same grace?*

Our end-of-life journey is a deeply emotional and spiritual experience, representing the culmination of our life's journey. As we approach this pivotal moment, it is essential to reflect on our lives and prepare ourselves for what is to come. For many years, death has been a taboo subject, and we have avoided discussing it. But as we become more aware of our spiritual journey and our connection to the divine, we are beginning to embrace the subject of death more openly. We recognize the importance of conversations about death and the need to approach this moment with grace and acceptance.

It can be challenging to talk about death, and we often feel uncomfortable or anxious when we do. However, if we can approach our own passing with the same purity, love, and confidence that we had when we were born, we can find peace in our final moments and ensure that our transition is a beautiful and sacred experience. As spiritual beings having a human experience, it is our birthright to approach our final journey with love, hope, and grace.

Similar to how we prepare for our legal and financial matters before death, it is important to view our energetic fields as requiring the same level of careful preparation. As spiritual beings, our desire is to ascend, and part of our journey involves transcending the situations we encounter throughout our lives.

The end-of-life journey is a sacred and deeply personal experience that requires the utmost care and compassion. As an energy healer and nurse, I feel privileged to accompany my clients on this journey and to witness their transformation and growth. When we can release the fear associated with this process, we are left with an incredibly profound and heart-opening experience. Just imagine being able to welcome the Light with open arms, free from fear!

Through our own experiences, we can help others find their way through the darkness. The inner light that shines from the core of our being is a beacon that guides us towards our true nature, values, and purpose. This divine spark or consciousness is inherent in every individual and serves as a source of wisdom, truth, and guidance. It illuminates the path forward and helps us find our way even in the darkest of times.

Our existence on this earth is merely a preparation for the ultimate transition - the Great Initiation - from this physical realm to the Beyond, a higher state of existence. Through death, we experience liberation from our physical bodies and embark on a new phase of spiritual evolution. This transition is a journey towards a higher state of consciousness or a reunion with the divine. It represents a return to our origins, to the divine union that we came from and to which we ultimately return.

Chapter Seventeen

UNCONDITIONAL LOVE

A s I soaked up the warmth of the sun, a sudden realization hit me hard - I had been guarding my heart closely, shielding it from the pain of my past. Though I allowed others to get close, I always held back, afraid of being abandoned and hurt again. My life experiences had taught me that amidst all the beauty, there was always pain lurking around the corner. However, by keeping my heart closed off, I was depriving myself of meaningful connections. As I began to heal and piece myself back together, I noticed that my defenses were slowly dropping, and I was shedding my mask. Through this inner work, my relationships and decisions started to shift. I understood that I was the only one capable of doing the work, and I had to be willing to take that step.

However, I wasn't alone. It took a community of support to help me through it. Healing wasn't a quick fix, but a gradual process of accepting help and delving deep within to find the sense of wholeness that was always there, beyond the pain. My healing team consisted of physiotherapists, acupuncturists, naturopaths, family physicians, surgeons, endocrinologists, counsellors, shamans, friends, family, and even energy healers. But it wasn't just physical and medical support that helped me heal. I also turned to meditation, prayer, and journaling to support my mental, emotional, and spiritual wellbeing. Building a consistent daily practice of mantra-based meditation played a crucial role in my comprehensive healing journey. Every aspect of healing, from physical to emotional to spiritual, needed attention and care.

As I began to open my heart, I saw positive changes in many of my close relationships with family and friends. My inner work served as a catalyst for healing in all of my relationships. I recognized that every change had to start with me.

As I transformed my own behaviors and patterns, those around me responded accordingly. Being a people pleaser for so long took a toll on me emotionally. I often found myself agreeing to things I didn't want to do just to avoid conflict and maintain a sense of harmony in my relationships. However, over time, I realized that my constant need to please others was causing me to neglect my own needs and desires. Saying "no" felt almost impossible at times, as I feared rejection and the potential for damaging the relationships I had worked so hard to maintain.

As I began to work on myself and prioritize my own well-being, I noticed a shift in the way I related to those around me. I started to recognize the importance of healthy boundaries in relationships, and that saying "no" when necessary was an act of self-care rather than a betrayal of my loved ones. This newfound sense of assertiveness allowed me to form deeper and more meaningful connections with the people in my life who respected and valued my authentic self.

I also noticed that as I evolved and grew, my friendships and relationships evolved with me. I started to resonate with people who shared similar values and perspectives, rather than trying to fit in with those who didn't align with my true self. While some relationships fell away, I found that the connections that remained were stronger and more fulfilling because they were based on mutual respect and understanding. Ultimately, learning to assert myself and set boundaries allowed me to experience deeper connections and greater emotional fulfillment in my relationships.

Eventually, I felt safe enough to get to the place where I could open my heart completely.

As I was able to open myself amidst the sorrow and pain, I learned I could meet others in healing from this new place of compassion and love. Healing empowered me to feel safe again and to be able to approach my relationships from an open-hearted and loving space instead of being rooted in fear and trauma. All the inner work and healing brought me to a level where I could create true intimacy within my closest relationships. Allowing myself to be loved granted an even deeper layer of healing to descend upon my entire being. Learning how to heal from that vulnerable space even allowed me to eventually fall in love and create a second chance at love.

Walking my spiritual path has been a transformative journey of self-discovery and growth. At first, I thought it was all about seeking enlightenment in a higher realm, but as I progressed, I realized that the real work was bringing that light and love into our physical world. It's about embodying our divine essence and making it a reality in our daily lives. It's a delicate balance between the spiritual and physical realms, a dance that requires mindfulness, intention, and courage.

As I worked on healing and integrating my broken pieces, I discovered the divinity within myself. It was a profound realization that shifted everything for me. I could finally recognize that same divinity in others, and it brought a whole new level of depth and connection to my relationships. I learned that in a relationship, we share our whole being, not just the light and loving parts, but also the messy emotions that make us human. It's about accepting and embracing all parts of ourselves, including the trauma and pain, with love and compassion.

Through this process, I created new experiences, memories, and patterns that aligned with my true essence. Even the most ordinary things felt extraordinary and sacred because I was living in a conscious and expanded space. As I shed the lower aspects of my personality and acknowledged my past mistakes and flaws, I could choose differently and create a new way of being that was in harmony with myself and my environment.

Living in acceptance and peace has been the most beautiful and rewarding part of this journey. No longer at war with myself or others, I've learned to trust the process of life and let go of control. It's a continuous journey of transformation and growth, and I am grateful every day for the power of conscious living.

Expanding my awareness and opening my heart has been a transformative journey, allowing me to see the world and myself in a new light. I now understand that vulnerability is not weakness, but rather a beautiful expression of strength and authenticity.

In a conscious relationship, there is a deep understanding that we are all interconnected, all integral pieces of a divine source. We see ourselves and our partners as more than just our personalities, but as spiritual beings on a shared path of growth and evolution. This awareness allows us to create a safe and nurturing space for both partners to thrive and flourish.

Open and honest communication is key in a conscious relationship, as we recognize that our emotions and feelings are valid and deserving of acknowledgement. We actively listen to our partners' needs and concerns, and conflict is viewed as an opportunity for growth and learning. Together, we work towards finding constructive solutions that honor each other's perspectives and needs.

Self-care and spiritual practices are also a priority in a conscious relationship. We understand that in order to be fully present and available for our partner, we must prioritize our own emotional and mental well-being. This involves engaging in practices that help us connect to our spiritual essence, as well as setting healthy boundaries to maintain a healthy balance between our individual needs and the needs of the relationship.

Through this expanded awareness, we can recognize the interconnectedness of all things and the divine force that guides us through life. We begin to see synchronicities and patterns in our experiences, opening us up to the power of the universe and the beauty of God.

Synchronicity is a profound manifestation of the interconnectedness and interdependence of all things in the universe. It suggests that there is an underlying order or pattern to our experiences that transcends the boundaries of time and space. When we experience synchronicity, we realize that there is something much larger and more mysterious at work in the world than we can perceive with our limited senses.

At its core, synchronicity is not just a coincidence, but a meaningful coincidence that carries a message or a lesson for us to learn. When we experience synchronicity, we may feel a sense of awe and wonder, as if we have been given a glimpse into a deeper reality beyond our ordinary perception.

The spiritual significance of synchronicity lies in its ability to awaken us to a deeper reality beyond our everyday experience. It can reveal that there is more to life than meets the eye and that our individual lives are part of a larger cosmic plan. When we experience synchronicity, we may feel a sense of interconnectedness and interdependence with all things, as if we are a small part of a larger whole.

Synchronicity can be seen as a call to awaken to our true nature and to align ourselves with the flow of life. By paying attention to the signs and symbols that appear in our lives, we can gain insight into our soul's purpose and the direction we need to take. Synchronicity can be a powerful tool for spiritual growth and self-discovery, as it can help us to understand our experiences and find meaning and purpose in our lives.

Ultimately, synchronicity is a reminder that we are not alone in our journey and that the universe is conspiring to help us fulfill our highest potential. When we open ourselves up to the mysteries of synchronicity, we can experience a deeper sense of connection to ourselves, to others, and to the world around us. We can learn to trust in the unfolding of life and to embrace the unknown with curiosity and wonder.

At a workshop in Ojai, California many years ago, every one of my senses became so completely overwhelmed with unconditional love it nearly paralyzed me. The enormous amount of light and love at that moment was so tremendous I became afraid that my container, my body, could not possibly hold that much light, and my hands began to contract and my legs unwilling to move. Trauma, pain and loss were what I was so accustomed to. My body wasn't familiar with how to react in the presence of such beauty and power. It felt like I would burst into a million pieces if I didn't tightly contain the vibration sweeping through my entire body.

That is what I had done my entire life. In the face of such enormous energy, I had always suppressed or contained my emotions. The fear of losing control paralyzed me because I was experiencing something beyond words and understanding. My mind raced, and my heart accelerated. I heard a faint whisper telling me everything was going to be ok. Consciously I acknowledged my fear and willed myself to surrender to a power far greater than myself. *Holy Mary, Mother of God, pray for us sinners now, and at the hour of our death*, I fervently prayed.

A part of me was dying.

But it was time for rebirth.

As I began to relax into the feeling of surrender, peace covered me as a blanket, and a feeling of deep communion with Spirit washed over me. I sensed the Master Healer, Jesus, present, emanating the pure essence of the Christ Light. He revealed to me His wounds and Sacred heart. Understanding, I opened my arms, welcoming His healing as His heart healed my own. My tears cleansed my soul, washing my spirit clean.

I was reminded that holding onto the trauma and grief was no longer necessary. I had become so accustomed to containing my suffering, but now, it was time to let it go. I remembered the feeling of unconditional love, belonging and worthiness, and it was time to reclaim what had always been mine.

I surrendered to the Light flowing into me.

Throughout the years, like a fortress, I had built protection barriers and hid behind masks, creating a container that trapped my essence. This container has represented a false safety based on fear. Courageously, I removed the lid, which had been tightly closed for many years. Acknowledging the suffering accumulated through time allowed all those dense emotions to rise and find liberation, no longer holding me hostage.

My soul knows there is so much more for me than what was inside the container. I asked myself *Who am I? Am I my container, my conditioning or something beyond all of that?* That container was only a result of conditioning, and I desired complete freedom from all limitations. And not only for that moment but for eternity. I came to the startling realization that it was entirely up to me to CHOOSE what I wanted to fill my being with from this point forward. The unconditional love the Universe so freely offers every single one of us was always waiting there for me to claim.

Joy and unconditional love are what I AM, I realized.

I didn't need to desire, earn or fight for it.

It is as it always was. Mine.

And so it is.

Chapter Eighteen

WHOLE

The sun beats down strongly, and my heels sink into the warm, soft earth. The air is still, bees hovering on the morning of Gabriel's 18th birthday. I'm walking through a redwood forest near Santa Cruz, California.

I stroll by a nearly 2,000-year-old Mother Tree, feeling peaceful, and lay my hand on her in a prayer of gratitude. Looking around this outdoor cathedral, my eyes search for a place to sit.

Moments before, I'd experienced a profound spiritual awakening. I viewed the world through unclouded eyes, a new lens; everything seemed vibrant, alive, fresh, and filled with wonder. Years of judgment, sorrow and unworthiness vanished, and I experienced the freedom to embrace my Creator's unconditional love. I felt complete unity with everything around me. I felt at peace. Finally.

I felt *home.*

Lying down on a long wooden bench in the quiet forest, I meditate on this experience. My eyes close, and my physical body drops away. And instantly, I am transported into a state of pure consciousness, what feels like a different dimension.

I see my precious Gabriel swinging in the forest.

When he sees me, Gabriel leaps down and runs to me as fast as his little legs can. He runs and falls into my arms and wraps himself around me, slathering my face in his kisses. *He's here. My little boy is here!* I have dreamed about holding him in my arms again. Now he cradles my face between his tiny hands, smiles and beams, "I love you!"

Compassionately I share my struggle with him. Gabriel tells me it's no longer necessary, that I've made him so proud, as he'd walked each step through grief beside me. Tenderly he kisses my tear-stained cheeks. As I hold him safely on my lap, an instant later, my little boy grows into an adult, tall, strong, and handsome. I stroke my finger down his cheek and look into his brilliant blue eyes—no longer the eyes of the small child I had lost. He's here now as my spirit guide.

Suddenly he fades away. My awareness returns to the hard wooden bench. My eyes are wet from joyful tears. How beautiful it felt to hold him in my arms, hear his voice, and feel his heart so near to mine. This was a gift I will treasure for the rest of my life.

The memory of my experience with Unity Consciousness remained with me, even as I faced the challenging moments that followed. Doubt, anger, self-criticism, and guilt threaten to overpower me at times, but I hold onto the memory of that profound state of awareness. It was a feeling of pure bliss and connectedness, a sensation of being one with all of existence. In that state, I felt an overwhelming sense of love and compassion for all living beings. It was a place of pure, unconditional love, where the boundaries between myself and the world around me dissolved into nothingness.

Though that state didn't last forever, it forever changed me. It opened me up to a deeper understanding of the interconnectedness of all things and sparked a longing within me to return to that state of being. I knew that this was the way to transcend my ego and connect with a higher source of wisdom and understanding. Through this experience, I came to understand that no matter how challenging life may be, the memory of that profound expansion could guide me towards inner peace, compassion, and a sense of interconnectedness with all of existence.

Through the pain of losing my Mom and Gabriel, I discovered hidden blessings that emerged from my grief. Even in the midst of loss, I realized that a boundless love still exists. There is no separation between us and our loved ones who have passed. Instead, we may experience moments where we feel their presence, like when we hear their favorite song or catch a whiff of their familiar perfume in the air. These signs serve as reminders that our loved ones are still with us, offering comfort in our times of need.

Despite the heartache, I realized that we are all part of a greater plan. By expanding our perspective, we can see the intricate blueprint of the universe woven throughout our lifetime, especially in the depths of our sorrow. With open eyes, we can witness the world as the Divine sees it and rediscover the sense of wonder and curiosity we had as children.

Grief may still overwhelm me at times, but I find strength in the joy that also exists within me. I remember feeling guilty the first time I laughed after Gabriel's passing, but now I understand that embracing happiness honors his soul. Despite the struggles, we are meant to live life to the fullest, to transform tragedy into something greater, and to pick ourselves up after every fall.

A few days later, basking in the sunshine under an enormous redwood tree, I placed my hands on my chest, feeling the rhythm of my heartbeat. I ponder each beat, how the heart represents life. Our circulatory system functions through complex and interconnected components, working in unison: arteries carrying oxygenated blood and then returning the oxygen-depleted blood back to the heart. *What incredible harmony!*

This is a direct reflection of my own being. I experienced multiple system failures on many levels due to the traumas I faced. Now I was finding harmony within my body, mind and spirit, repairing each part of the working system.

Every second of every day of my life, my heart beats. No conscious effort is needed to make it happen; it just *happens*.

When I close my heart, I shut off the flow of love. Keeping my heart open, despite multiple losses, I transformed the pain and suffering into the willpower to continue, the strength to walk forward, and the courage to find a bridge over that pain.

The heart is our bridge between the Divine and the Earth, our higher and lower selves. Because of our hearts, we hold the divine capacity for compassion, forgiveness, and love. The heart connects people by showing empathy, kindness, and compassion, creating meaningful connections. Emotionally, it can help bridge the gap between our emotions and rational thinking by allowing us to experience our feelings fully. Our hearts can also link our past and future by reflecting on our experiences and using the lessons learned to build a better future. Physically, the heart serves as a bridge within our bodies by pumping blood throughout our circulatory system, ensuring that our organs and systems function properly and helping us maintain optimal health and well-being.

Now I was experiencing something beyond words and understanding. Under the redwood tree, as I began to relax into the feeling of surrender, peace covered me like a blanket, and a sense of deep communion with Spirit washed over me. I sensed the Master Healer, Jesus, was present, emanating the pure essence of the Christ Light. He revealed His wounds and sacred heart, urging me to reclaim what had always been mine.

I surrendered to the Light flowing into me. As the Light entered, an entirely new world opened. I lifted my arms, welcoming healing, strength, courage, and an embrace from the Divine.

Broken but whole.

Heart wide open.

Awakened.

Chapter Nineteen

AN EPIC LIFE

Despite the pain, guilt, shame and suffering that we may experience, it's important to remember that we are so much more than our broken hearts. We have the right to create an epic life, one that is filled with joy, purpose and meaning. We can ask ourselves, "Who can I be beyond this pain and suffering?" and explore the many facets of our identity that extend beyond our current struggles. It's an opportunity for us to discover the sacred within the mundane and to recognize the extraordinary within the ordinary.

The experiences we have throughout our lives can leave us with emotional burdens and dense energies, but it's essential to recognize that these are not a reflection of our true selves. If we were able to view ourselves through the template of perfection, we would no longer feel weighed down by the traumas and hardships we've endured. Life is a constant cycle of evolution, and within this cycle, there is a natural order to birth, life and death. However, dying isn't limited to just physical death. Throughout our lifetime, we may experience various layers of death within ourselves. Through our inner work, we can shed these layers and experience a rebirth, where we feel the heavens open up to us and we are born anew.

With each time that we work through our deeper and denser emotions, we transmute the negative energies into a higher vibration of unconditional love. When we reflect on our lives from a different perspective, we can observe both subtle and significant changes in our demeanor. As we grow and evolve, our consciousness expands, and we become more aligned with our true selves. Every one of us has the potential to navigate through life's challenges and unexpected events. We are not confined or stuck in any situation. The choice to move forward and grow is ultimately ours to make. By taking responsibility for our part in the process and aligning our physical, mental, emotional and spiritual bodies, we can begin the healing journey and enter into the flow of life's current.

As humans, we have the ability to create our own circumstances despite our emotional and physical scars.

Brokenness, rejection, grief; these emotional scars are universal. No one escapes them; no one can hide from them, and there is no way around them. We can only go *through them*. Whether it's a lost job, a broken relationship, or the death of a loved one, each human being faces them and must grapple with the eternal question:

What is my purpose?

Brokenness can lead to an awakening, a revelation. It can inspire growth in so many ways. Dealing with brokenness is a question of choice. We can choose to confront our doubts and approach every struggle with an open heart—or we can dodge that path and blame ourselves and others. When we face difficulty, our instincts tell us to close our hearts, protect ourselves from future pain, and hide or run away. Brokenness can leave us feeling separated. We can fall into the illusion that we are all alone in our pain. We close our hearts so that we don't experience further hurt. When our hearts are closed, we deprive ourselves of giving, feeling, and being loved.

Yet brokenness is also an opportunity to clear the past and create a clean slate. To approach each moment, each day, each breath as something holy, something new.

The journey of healing has been a challenging path. The road has been a non-stop route of unexpected pit stops and surprise curves, and it has been a path of accelerating and then braking hard. But keeping that forward momentum was always pivotal with each obstacle and hurdle faced.

Whenever faced with obstacles, I was presented with a choice: to move forward with faith and love or to succumb to fear and retreat. Throughout my healing journey, I had to tap into that internal driving force, time and time again, to propel me to the next level. It took me a while to realize that I was never taking a step backwards. Instead, I was moving forward by processing and working through deeper levels of the pain and suffering I had endured. I constantly drew upon the I AM force deep within my essence, even when I didn't fully understand what I was experiencing. Through trust and reliance on my innate knowledge, I knew that I was equipped to handle every challenge that came my way.

Shining a flashlight on the deepest, darkest parts of our own internal struggle is no easy task. Healing requires fortitude, courage and tenacity. It demands of us flexibility, willingness and surrender. But overcoming these challenges reminds us that we would not find our strength without struggle. We would not recognize triumph without first experiencing failure. The depths to which we are willing to delve are proportionate to the heights we can soar.

Even if I had foreseen the sorrow and pain that life would bring me, I would still choose to live it all over again. As strange as it may sound, those experiences have taught me about the depth of my being. Each time I encounter grief and loss, I am reminded of the joy that bubbles within me. Because I have experienced profound sorrow, I now know the exquisite joy in the simplest moments. It is because of the moments when I was on my knees, heart shattered on the ground, that I know what it means to have unwavering faith. I am grateful for having had the opportunity to love so fully and completely that I know the pain of loss. This has taught me to cherish every moment, to never take anything for granted and to remember that tomorrow is never promised.

The key to living a fulfilling life is to remain present in each moment. By staying in the present, our past no longer has a hold on us, and we are no longer fearful of the future. When we are fully present in every snapshot of time, we can experience the richness of our human existence without being biased by our past or future. This way, we can remain grateful with open hearts, welcoming every experience, knowing that we are fully equipped to handle anything that comes our way.

The flow of emotions is akin to that of a river. Just as water shapes the river bank over time, our emotions shape our thoughts and behaviors. Sometimes emotions seem to dry up, leaving us feeling disconnect and empty. At other times, they can flood our being, causing destruction and chaos. Yet, like a river, emotions can also be incredibly beautiful and profound, revealing hidden depths within us. As we navigate our healing journey, we are like the river, bridging the gap between our current state and our spiritual selves. By surrendering to the power within and far beyond us and expanding our awareness, we can find true peace and become whole, like a river flowing into the vastness of the ocean.

Tapping into Source, accessing that peace, compassion and love, that feeling of being completely held by Spirit, is where I found my true self. And where you, too, can find yourself. That is the most extraordinary gift.

Our circumstances can often make us feel trapped, and its natural to perceive life as a version of Hell on Earth. We experience doubt, fear, shame, guilt and a range of other emotions, making our suffering seem unbearable. However, once we work through this suffering and begin to overcome it, we can start to embody divine qualities that bring us closer to experiencing Heaven on Earth. Ultimately, our spiritual journey leads us back Home, which is not a physical place.

We have all the tools necessary within to create the world around us that resonates with us. Heaven and Hell are right here, right now, at this moment, and it's only a question of where we are on our journey.

We have a responsibility to collect the broken pieces of ourselves, grind them down to dust and then mix them with gold and love, which acts as the glue that fuses our fractured vessel back together. Every step of remembering brings us back to wholeness. From this space, wherever you look, you find yourself, the beauty of God's creation and the embodiment of love. The golden bonds of unconditional love continuously flow, providing an abundance of forgiveness and compassion to share with others on our journey.

Reflecting upon my healing journey and standing where I am today, I cannot conceive of the mysterious force that has guided me through each step and difficult decision. I humbly bow in honor and awe to this Power.

That same power is also in you. Find it, and wherever you look, you, too, will experience that same force.

That life force is what guides us through the steady and never-ending stream of each and every experience. Slowing down brings us back to where we began, as creations of a loving God.

Each of us is like a rose, perfect in design. As a result of our hurt, we develop our own thorns as layers of protection. Sometimes it's difficult to see the beauty when we constantly focus on the thorns, and we forget that we are so much more than that. Our perspective distorts until all we can see is the trauma, the pain, and the suffering. As we tend to the thorns, pruning them away, we catch a glimpse of the beautiful bud we began life as. As we release our defensive behaviors and begin to open our hearts, we unfold like a gorgeous blossoming rose, remembering our own pure essence.

Epilogue

INNER TEMPLE

M y hope is that by sharing my experiences, thoughts, and voice with courage, I can inspire you to overcome your own battles with loss, grief, or trauma. Even if it's just one small change in your life today, I believe it can make a significant difference in your journey toward healing and growth.

Life is a process of becoming; I'm excited for all we are to become.

We came here to remember and live our Divine union. As we heal ourselves, we heal the world, and healing ourselves brings us on a return path to Oneness with the Light. We discover the power to heal ourselves because the Divine is within each one of us.

As I ponder on my own life's journey, I am filled with a deep sense of appreciation and wonder for the myriad of experiences that have enriched my soul. In churches around the globe, I have been reminded of the power of faith and the interconnectedness of all things. My journeys have also taken me to the heart of nature, where I have witnessed the wisdom and majesty of the natural world, reminding me of the interconnectedness of all things and our place in the grand scheme of things.

Through these experiences, I have come to realize the importance of cultivating a deep spiritual connection with something greater than ourselves. Whether it be through prayer, meditation, or simple contemplation, it is through this connection that we tap into the infinite wisdom and potential within ourselves.

Ultimately, all of this has brought me to a profound realization: that our existence is a tapestry of experiences, each one a thread that weaves together the fabric of our being. And it is through embracing these experiences, both light and dark, that we can fully appreciate the beauty and richness of life.

I've held my newborn babies with reverence and awe of God's incredible creation and blessing, filled with an immense sense of gratitude and wonder for the divine creation that lay before me. In their tiny, delicate forms, I saw the infinite potential of life and the preciousness of each moment. As I gazed into their innocent eyes, I felt a deep connection to the divine and an overwhelming sense of love and protection. Holding them close, I knew that these tiny beings were not just my children, but spiritual beings on a journey of their own. With each breath they took, I felt the universe expand and contract, and I was humbled by the magnitude of it all. In those moments, I knew that my purpose was to guide them and help them grow into their fullest potential, while also learning from the wisdom and purity that they brought into my life.

Looking into the eyes of my Beloved, I felt a love so profound and all-encompassing that it brought tears to my eyes. It was a love that transcended all boundaries and limitations, a love that existed beyond time and space. In this love, there was no fear, no judgment, no separation. It was a love that embraced all, unconditionally.

All of these experiences have expanded my awareness and deepened my connection to the world around me. I am grateful for each one, and I look forward to continuing my journey of exploration and discovery.

As I reflect on my journey through life, I am filled with an overwhelming sense of gratitude and emotion. The experiences and lessons I have gained have touched me deeply, leaving an indelible mark on my soul.

I am grateful for the countless moments of beauty and wonder that I have witnessed, for the people who have touched my life and for the love that has surrounded me in all its forms. I am grateful for the challenges and struggles that have taught me resilience and inner strength, and for the moments of pure joy that have made my heart sing.

Through all the highs and lows, I have learned to trust in the journey and to embrace each moment with an open heart and mind. True wisdom comes not from what we acquire, but from what we give back to the world.

As I move forward on my path, I carry with me the lessons learned, the love shared, and the hope for a better tomorrow. And I know that, wherever my journey takes me, I will always be guided by the light of my own inner temple, and the infinite potential that lies within each and every one of us.

Delve deeply into your inner temple and embrace the beauty of your essence. Allow the radiant Light that burns within your core to expand and emanate love and compassion into the world. As you let your inner Light shine, you inspire those around you to do the same.

You are made of the stars, a child of the Universe. When you feel broken and alone, know deeply that you are an integral part of the working Whole. You are not alone.

May your journey be filled with wondrous healing and abundance,
May you nurture compassion and love for yourself and all others,
May you discover peace and beauty in every facet of your life,
And may you walk with the innocent and joyful heart of a child,
Eagerly taking each step with eyes full of wonder.

~ Love, Christy

Acknowledgements

To my teacher, Deborah King, I am deeply grateful for the powerful reminder you have given me that true healing comes from within. Your guidance has helped me rediscover my authentic self. Infinite gratitude for your wisdom and love.

I also want to express my heartfelt appreciation to all the mentors and spiritual teachers over the years who have graced my life with their presence. Your unwavering support and wisdom have been instrumental in my personal growth and transformation. Thank you for your unconditional love and for holding space for me on this journey.

To all my Soul family and all the incredible healers I am blessed to know: Thank you for supporting me, holding me up and surrounding me with unconditional love throughout this healing journey.

Cat, what would I do without your love and friendship? This book would not be what it is—nor would I. Thank you for your invaluable insights and inspiration!

Kim, you know me inside and out, and I'm so grateful to have found deep understanding and sisterhood for life!

JoAnne, thank you for always being in my corner and supporting and loving me as your own. You are such a blessing in my life!!

Carlene, you've been there through it ALL—my best friend since birth. I love you!

Papa, you have been a constant support in my life. I'm grateful for your love and for teaching me always to follow my intuition. Without you, none of this would have been possible. Thank you for believing in me!

To my beautiful daughters Micah and Annika, thank you for the joy, love and light you bring to my life! I love you to the moon and back!

My beloved husband, Vedran, infinite love and gratitude for loving me through the peaks and the valleys these past couple of years, especially while devoting myself to this labor of love. Your support, unconditional love and ability to hold me through it all leaves me in awe.

I am blessed!

About the Author

Always attuned to the compassionate heart from a young age, Christy Droog felt led toward a career in the healing arts. Her journey began with the pursuit of a Bachelor's Degree in Nursing, paving the way for a remarkable 20-year journey as a Registered Nurse with a special focus on palliative care.

Life's hardships deepened Christy's search for purpose. Overcoming the heart-wrenching loss of her young son in a drowning and the passing of her mother due to cancer, she embarked on a quest for greater meaning. This journey led her to the Deborah King Center, where she encountered holistic healing modalities that seamlessly united mind, body, and soul.

Fuelled by an unwavering passion for the subtle yet potent realm of energy healing, Christy's exploration took an exponential leap. She delved into the intricacies of chakras and the human energy field, discovering their pivotal role in our inherent well-being. These teachings unveiled the art of connecting with Source, enabling her to harness and channel energy to aid others in their profound journey of healing and transformation.

A graduate of Deborah's LifeForce Energy Healing® Masters Program, Christy remains steadfast in her commitment to growth. She continuously hones her expertise as a certified practitioner, Vedic Meditation Teacher, and Senior Grad Teacher at the Deborah King Center as well as an inspirational speaker.

For more insights into Christy's transformative work and ways to reach her: www.christydroog.com.

Book Endorsements

"In *Broken Whole*, Christy showcases an exceptional talent for capturing the intricate emotions and the delicate path of personal reconstruction after trauma. Christy offers solace and instills hope, unveiling the profound impact of self-discovery and self-acceptance as catalysts for transformation."

–Sarah Michelle Wergin, RN LAC

"With grace and vulnerability, Christy shares her own experiences of grief and loss. Her powerful words illuminate the path to finding light amid the darkness, offering solace, hope, and inspiration to those who have endured their own trials. *Broken Whole* is a must-read for anyone seeking healing and transformation in the face of adversity."

–Cathy Gabrielsen, #1 bestselling author of
Dying to Live: Surviving Near-Death

"In life, you are truly blessed to come across these precious souls that co-create Heaven on Earth. As an Interfaith Minister, I know Our Creator very well and what I know for sure—God sends Angels Like Christy Droog to remind us all that we are loved no matter what! 'Thank you!' Christy for blessing the world with a piece of Heaven with your beautiful truth-filled book!"

–Rev. Dr Paul Luftenegger, International Singer and Songwriter